Praise for *Office Mons*

CW00665832

'Imagination and interdisciplinary
managers. The intersection of ma............ ... .
out to be a powerful combination. Highly recommended reading and
viewing.'

**Prof Dr Sarah Lubik, Head of Innovation, Simon Fraser
University, Beedie School of Business**

'You don't need be afraid of office monsters anymore. Whether they
lurk inside you, dwell within others, or even if they spread their tentacles across your organisation, you can tame them, slay them, or make
friends, with this handy field guide by Martin J. Eppler and Andri
Hinnen.'

**Dave Gray, bestselling author of *Gamestorming*; founder,
The School of the Possible**

'Being a (what I thought pretty decent) author myself, the sheer
brilliance and creativity of this book, and Andri's and Martin's skill to
turn the corporate world into a fun and adventurous place, definitely
unleashed my own Sirens of Self- doubt!'

Mats Frey, Netflix writer (*How to Sell Drugs Online (Fast)*)

'How many monsters are inside you? An amusing and, unfortunately,
not untrue book helping you exorcise your workplace.'

**Roman Tschäppeler, author of *The Collaboration Book*, and
many other international bestsellers.**

'A monstrous book - funny AND useful.'

Pablo Koerfer, CEO, Farner Group

'This book is an absolute delight to read. The mix of humour, anecdotes and real-world examples makes it a true page-turner, offering both entertainment and valuable insights into modern management. Highly recommended!'

Jörg Schulze, film producer/creative producer
(*The Happy Prince, Guns Akimbo, The Crow*)

Office Monsters

Pearson

At Pearson, we have a simple mission: to help people make more of their lives through learning.

We combine innovative learning technology with trusted content and educational expertise to provide engaging and effective learning experiences that serve people wherever and whenever they are learning.

From classroom to boardroom, our curriculum materials, digital learning tools and testing programmes help to educate millions of people worldwide – more than any other private enterprise.

Every day our work helps learning flourish, and wherever learning flourishes, so do people.

To learn more, please visit us at **www.pearson.com**

Office Monsters

A survival guide to
corporate madness

Martin J. Eppler
Andri Hinnen

Pearson

Harlow, England • London • New York • Boston • San Francisco • Toronto • Sydney
Dubai • Singapore • Hong Kong • Tokyo • Seoul • Taipei • New Delhi
Cape Town • São Paulo • Mexico City • Madrid • Amsterdam • Munich • Paris • Milan

PEARSON EDUCATION LIMITED
KAO Two
KAO Park
Harlow CM17 9NA
United Kingdom
Tel: +44 (0)1279 623623
Web: www.pearson.com

First edition published 2025 (print and electronic)

ISBN: 978-1-292-47047-4 (print)
          978-1-292-73851-2 (ePub)

British Library Cataloguing-in-Publication Data
A catalogue record for the print edition is available from the British Library

Library of Congress Cataloging-in-Publication Data
Names: Eppler, Martin J., 1971- author. | Hinnen, Andri, 1985- author.
Title: Office Monsters : a survival guide to corporate madness /
    Martin J. Eppler, Andri Hinnen.
Description: First edition. | Harlow, England ; New York : Pearson, 2025. |
    Includes bibliographical references and index.
Identifiers: LCCN 2024036549 | ISBN 9781292470474 (paperback) | ISBN
    9781292738512 (epub)
Subjects: LCSH: Psychology, Industrial. | Work--Psychological aspects. |
    Managing your boss. | Career development.
Classification: LCC HF5548.8 .E67 2025 | DDC 158.7--dc23/eng/20240920
LC record available at https://lccn.loc.gov/2024036549

10 9 8 7 6 5 4 3 2 1
29 28 27 26 25

Cover design by Two Associates

All illustrations in this book are by Felipe Vasconcelos Torres

Print edition typeset in 10/14 Charter ITC Pro by Straive
Printed and bound by CPI Group (UK) Ltd, Croydon, CR0 4YY

NOTE THAT ANY PAGE CROSS REFERENCES REFER TO THE PRINT EDITION

Contents

——

Contents

About the authors

Martin J. Eppler, PhD, grew up in an information junkie household with more than 20 magazine subscriptions and a two-room library, so he wrote a 400-page dissertation on information overload (talk about embracing paradox) and is now the most cited researcher in the world on the topic. Since then, he has shifted from the problem to the solution and has conducted more than 40 projects (many experimental) on how visualisation can overcome overload and convey knowledge effectively in his role as chaired Professor of Communication at the University of St. Gallen.

He is the author of more than 200 academic papers and 24 books, several of which have won awards such as 'International Business Book of the Year', 'HR Book of the Year' and 'Career Book of the Year'. He has won numerous best papers and teaching awards, and his research has been featured in *Inc. Magazine*, the *Harvard Business Review*, TED.com, *Bloomberg Businessweek*, the *MIT Technology Review* and others. He is the inventor of the periodic table of visualisation methods, the let's-focus software suite, the synergy map method and the nudging approach to meetings. In addition to his university role (where he led an MBA programme for many years), he is an advisor to organisations such as the United Nations, the European Central Bank, Porsche, Swiss Re, the Anti-Tobacco Fund, Salesforce and others. He's been a guest professor at institutions such as Cambridge University, Georgia Tech, Simon Fraser University and CUFE Beijing.

Andri Hinnen holds a BA in International Relations and a double masters in Strategy and International Management (SIM/CEMS). He co-founded Zense, a consultancy and agency specialising in complexity and change communication (zense.ch). He has worked with global brands like Coca-Cola, Lufthansa and UBS, visualising their strategies and instilling corporate cultures with sense, sensibility and a bit of nonsense. He is a regular lecturer at the University of St. Gallen on reframing complexity, storytelling, visualisation and sensemaking.

Andri is also a filmmaker and author. His documentary feature *Breathing Underwater* won the Zurich Film Festival and was acquired by Netflix. Together with his brother, Gieri Hinnen, he wrote the German non-fiction bestsellers *Reframe It* and *Change It*. His personalised children's book *Welcome to the World* has sold over 100,000 copies and has been translated into several languages. In 2021, Andri's first novel *Rolf* was published and is currently being adapted into a feature film. In 2024, Andri was chosen as Personality in Residence at HSG-Square. Among Andri's favourite mythical creatures are dragons, giants and cats.

Acknowledgements

Office-Monstrology is best conducted in groups. We would like to express our deepest gratitude to our fellow slayers, tamers and supporters, particularly. . .

Felipe Vasconcelos Torres for the beautiful and spirited illustrations.

Eleanna Zarn, for all the organisational support.

Eloise Cook, Yashmeena Bisht, Dhanya Ramesh and the rest of the Pearson bunch for guiding us through the thicket of global publishing.

Markus Aeschimann, for the brilliant Project Zombie idea.

All the Zense and MCM clients, for always inspiring us with your own stories of corporate monsters.

Dave Gray, for your valuable tips and introductions.

Gieri Hinnen and Peter Hinnen, for your unwavering support, humour and great ideas.

Monika Reller, for teaching us that many monsters need not be slain but studied and befriended.

Stephanie Motz, for that one clever input with the 'Yes to yourself' and for having been a great co-slayer for such a long time.

Angela Meraviglia, for being the perfect test-reader, full of joy and wit and positive energy.

The University of St Gallen for granting us a sabbatical in Monsterville.

And you, our readers, for your time, joy, interest and feedback. We sincerely hope we have made this read worth your while.

Introduction

'Heroes need monsters to establish their heroic credentials.'

Margaret Atwood

Dear Work Slayer and Office Warrior,

Welcome to the ultimate field guide to surviving corporate madness. You are about to learn about the 'office monsters', gruelling creatures found in meeting rooms, management floors, cubicle farms, in canteens and even in your own head. They love to attack individual careers, relationships or projects, and have the power to bring down entire organisations.

You've probably encountered them before on your adventurous quest to the top – or wherever you are heading. Without you realising it, a Yes Yeti might have whispered some icy yeses into your ears, tampering with your focus and leading you to take on too many tasks. Perhaps a Bureaucracy Beast is suffocating your company's entrepreneurial spirit at this very moment. Or did the buzzing Fad Fairies turn your critical mind into a gullible fan of the latest management trend? Is that why you bought *this* book? Oh boy.

Chances are, of course, that you have no idea what we are talking about. As many studies* have shown, our brains work overtime to shield us from the workplace horrors unfolding right before our eyes. But ignoring a problem rarely makes it go away. Quite the opposite: the more we let these monsters go about their business, the more they meddle with ours.

This is why everyone who wants a shot at a decent career in any office environment needs to train their brain to see that environment for what it really is: a place inhabited by monsters. Soon, you will see them everywhere. There will even come a time when you'll wish you had never bought this book at all. Feelings of existential dread and being overwhelmed by the many now-clearly-visible monsters will wash over you. But we assure you, it will pass. Ultimately, *Office Monsters* will help you thrive at work and pursue the career of your dreams.

To get down to business, this book will enable you to do three things:

1 **Recognise and resolve recurring (problematic) patterns at work:** We help you see work-related challenges for what they really are: tangible creatures in flesh and blood. This will make it easier for you to identify and tackle them. Think of it like using metaphors to reframe complex issues that are otherwise hard to grasp. Only this time, of course, it's real.

2 **Improve communication and collaboration:** *Office Monsters* will introduce you to a secret language that, up to this point, has only been spoken by an exclusive circle of office-space monster slayers. This will help you address and discuss issues with colleagues, bosses, friends and enemies. Some of them will laugh thinking that you are joking. Of course, this is only to your advantage as humour is known to be a powerful technique for relieving tension and facilitating communication. Only deep down you will always know: it is funny because it's true.

---

* Most of these studies are neither scientific nor real, of course. Okay, none of them are. Does this make them less true? Yes, it does. But as is well known, a story does not have to be true, but only to ring true. And that's what this is about. All of it.

3 **Expand your toolbox and explore new paths:** Finally,
   whether addressing challenges with a difficult colleague or
   breaking free from an innovation drought, looking beyond
   the grey facades of the 'normal' office world and exploring the
   monstrous pits that lurk beneath will enable you to envision
   new pathways for your heroic journey. We will also equip you
   with powerful spells and weapons to slay it at work. Can you
   muster the courage to use them?

And for all that to happen, you must read this book. There really is
no other option. Ideally, you read it five times, take it to work and
tell everyone about it. Unless you want to fall victim to the truly
dreadful and monstrous forces of corporate madness.

How this book is organised

The main part of this book is dedicated to the monsters that you
will inevitably face (off) at work. We believe in cleaning up our own
backyards first and spotting the monsters *inside* of you, which is why
we begin with the monsters within us. These 'Crippling creatures of
self-sabotage' live within us and are part of our psyche. They love
to curtail our productivity, creativity and communication skills.
Whether it's the mystical yet all-too-real Yes Yeti or the infamous
Anxiety Alien, the monsters within us demand mindfulness, self-
reflection and the courage to change.

We proceed to take a closer look at our creepy colleague creatures, or 'Monsters in others': they are seemingly inconspicuous
coworkers who let their behaviours not only harm their own careers,
but yours too. You will learn, for instance, about the Groupthink
Goblins, who dismiss every opinion other than their own as
ridiculous, or the Politicoraptor, a fierce and career-driven collegial
creature.

Finally, we take a closer look at 'Cursed corporate creatures'.
These organisational monsters do not hide behind individual human
beings. They haunt entire divisions, processes or buildings. Just wait

until you hear about the Strategy Chimera or the Project Zombie. Horrifying stuff.

In each of the 25 chapters, we begin with a brief interview snippet from an experienced work slayer. They are all veterans who have seen things you would not believe. Their trauma is our treasure, because oh, do they have stories to tell! At the beginning of each chapter you will also find a small information box that describes the monster and its taming in a nutshell.

We then talk about each monster in detail, describing habitat, appearance, behaviour and other relevant facts and figures.

From there we move on to equipping you with the necessary tools to deal with the monster in focus. Obviously, we want to teach you not only how to identify, but also how to master them. As you'll discover, each monster requires a different approach. Some leave you with only one option: show no mercy and slay them with all your might and fury. Others can be tamed and domesticated, if you are tenacious enough. And eventually, there are monsters that can become your friends, allies and, if you are into that sort of thing – we're not here to judge – lovers.

Finally, for the true monster nerds among our readers, we provide additional background information (Origins) and tips for further reading (Further reading).

After this main part, you will find a section preparing you for your own monster-bound excursions. Do you have what it takes to discover creatures that no one has ever seen before? Do you have the guts to build or breed monsters in your own lab? Having read Chapter 4, you will be ready to embark on your own slaying adventures.

We leave you with an outlook and a call to arms in the Epilogue. And now let the madness begin.

Oh, one more thing. We forgot to introduce ourselves – apologies. Our names are Martin and Andri. By day, Martin is a business school professor and Andri is the founder of a creative agency. But at night! Okay to be fair, we usually sleep at night. We are too cowardly to go out and hunt monsters ourselves. But we are fans of those who do. Which is why over the last decade we have indulged in every possible scroll of famous monster hunters we could get our hands on. Whether it's the poetic work of Prof. Sir Sinclair Slaysalot, the cryptic but brilliant descriptions in the oeuvre of Prof. Lady Dr Carla Young, the hands-on guidebooks of Mr Scrooge McKinsey himself or Petra Pen's amazing work with N.O.F.A.D. (National Organisation for the Fight Against Daftness) – all of them have become our teachers, and we are so grateful for that. All *we* did was collect, summarise and make this precious body of knowledge available to you, dearest reader.

And *now*, let the madness begin.

Martin and Andri
June 2024

Chapter 1

The monsters within you: Crippling creatures of self-sabotage

'The scariest monsters are the ones that lurk within our souls.'

Edgar Allen Poe

Our guide to the world of office monsters begins with a group of monsters that you know all too well, if you're willing to face them. We are talking about those creatures within you, scary monsters that are part of our psyche, soul and work habits. Some of them lead us astray from working well, thinking straight and being productive. Others torture us with self-doubt or fool us with illusions of superiority. If you tame these monsters within you, you will already have completed a third of your hero's journey to slaying it at work.

So be brave and meet the Yes Yeti, 'the Time Trolls', 'the Sirens of Self-doubt' or the Bias Basilisks. Last but not least, be ready to awaken the Mighty Me Monsters, powerful allies that help you achieve the career you have always dreamed of – or at least lead a good life.

The Yes Yeti

A friendly 'No' is mightier than the sword

> 'The Yes Yeti made me say yes to everything. At first,
> I believed it wanted to help me. But with every yes that
> I muttered out there in the cold, the Yeti got bigger. Eventually,
> it blocked my path to the peak. My breakthrough moment
> came when I discovered an ancient spell called the "Friendly
> No". It melted away all my sorrows and freed my way.'
>
> Dr Laura Frostblade
> National Organisation for Polite Empowerment (N.O.P.E.)

Yes Yetis can be encountered anywhere in the wild world of work –
at the office, at home, in airport lounges, board rooms and even
playgrounds. They make you say 'yes' to new tasks, favours or just
one more project. Maybe your colleague asks you to assist them
with a presentation, or your boss to review his report over the
weekend. The Yes Yeti will whisper in your ear with its icy voice,
'You can't let that opportunity slide. You gotta be nice to be loved.
You have to put yourself out there to climb the ladder. Do you really
want to offend Carl?'

And say 'yes', you will – yes to that, yes to this, yes to more than
you can chew. This is how you feed your Yeti. But be warned: when
you first meet it, your Yeti will not look menacing. One victim
reportedly said, 'At first, I just thought of it as a cute little fur ball.
Like a teddy that was looking out for me! It promised me all the
attention I deserved. How could I have been so wrong?'

Alas, with each 'yes' that escapes your lips, your Yeti will get
bigger until one day, without you realising, it becomes a monstrous
giant blocking your way. It is too late now. All the yeses have created a backlog that seems impossible to clear, and the more you
think about all your tasks, the more difficult the actual thinking
becomes.

Name:	Yes Yeti
Scientific name:	*Sic Bestia Nivis*
Function:	Makes work slayers say yes to too many things
Habitat:	Predominantly lower and middle management
Monstrosity level:	Moderate
Monster category:	Internal (may also manifest in colleagues)
Feeds on:	Altruism, ambition, lack of focus
Approach:	Tame it and let it out sparingly
Effective weapon:	The 'Friendly No' spell

How to master it

You need to tame your inner Yes Yeti, now. The key is to do so while
the Yeti is still small (the Spanish word for this is *Yetito*). Once the
creature has reached its full size, there is hardly any chance of
defeating it. All you can do then is clean up after its mess and pray
it will not whisper any more of those icy yeses into your ears. Of
course, you can always quit your job, change cities or spend some
quality time in a burnout clinic. This may contain your Yeti for a
while. But at what cost?

No, better get ahold of your Yes Yeti while it is still small.

Whenever someone approaches you with a task, think twice if
it is alright. Whether it is a colleague, a friend, your pet, your boss
or Carl, take a minute to reflect if the task is consistent with your
duties, priorities and values, as well as with your time and energy
constraints.

If it is not, then train yourself in the ancient art of the 'friendly no'.

'No' is *the* most powerful spell in history, but uttering it in an
unfriendly manner can be dangerous. If you are not careful, a
brusque 'no' can damage your relationships or reputation. So, try
saying it nicely rather than icily. Dress your 'no' up in sentences such
as the following:

- 'I would love to. But honestly, I am swamped. I really do not
  have the time right now to deliver the quality a project like this
  deserves.'

- 'I really care about you and your work. But if you do not do this
  yourself, you will not be able to do a good follow-up later on, don't
  you think?'

- 'Wow! Thanks for thinking of me regarding this task. But I must
  focus on a key priority of mine right now. I hope you understand.'

- 'I'll gladly give you feedback, but I feel I shouldn't be doing this
  myself. It should reflect who you are, and only you can do it in
  your way.'

- 'Sorry if I have to decline. I really must finish another task at
  this time.'

- 'This sounds amazing. But I am afraid if I say yes, I will not be able to keep my promise.'
- 'This is an important task. And I feel that I will not have the focus and dedication that it requires.'

You will see – the more you cast one of these nice 'no's upon your pursuers, the smaller your Yes Yeti gets. But please do not stop listening to your Yeti altogether. Saying 'yes' is like salt. You need it, but too much of it will kill you. And whenever you are hesitant about casting a friendly 'no', you can also think about it as a Yes to yourself: 'No thanks, I don't have the energy and the time for this project' – and yes to my own health, well-being and focus.

Origins

Research on the negative side effects of saying 'yes' too often is extensive. Most productivity guides contain advice such as, 'Be careful what you take on as additional tasks', 'Keep your focus by saying no', and 'Only say yes to what matters most'.

In a management context, the Yes Yeti is also known as *monkey management*, where you take on the tasks of your subordinates (as a monkey on your back) instead of empowering them to do them on their own.

One recent approach to nice but firm 'no's is called *empowered refusal* by U.S. business professor Vanessa Patrick. She suggests that to tame the Yes Yeti, you have to set up a few firm rules about what and when you accept tasks from others. For example, 'I will not start a new project until I finish an old one.' According to Patrick, you need to be crystal clear about your own identity, values and priorities and convert them into simple rules. Only say 'yes' to tasks that align with those rules and respond with a friendly but firm 'no' to all others.

Further reading

Patrick, V. (2023) *The Power of Saying No*. Sourcebooks.

Schlund, R., Sommers, R. and Bohns, V. K. (2024) 'Giving people the words to say no leads them to feel freer to say yes', *Scientific Reports*, 14, 576.

The Time Trolls

Terminating time thieves with a ticker

'Sneaky creatures! They seem cute at first, but I learned the hard way that they are everything but. When it comes to paralysing your progress, they are worse than the Sirens of Self-doubt. The trick is not to feed them with your precious time, but to beat them with a timer: set a 5-minute minimum to attack your most daunting challenges and a 20-minute timer for tasks that require undivided attention. This usually drives those trolls away. But be careful. They are easily startled, but they'll soon be back, and in greater numbers.'

Professor Sir Sinclair Slaysalot
Institute of Management for Productivity
and Creature Taming (I.M.P.A.C.T.)

Is your task list longer than Rapunzel's hair? Your mail piled higher than Jack's beanstalk? And all you want is to get things *done*? Oh, the time trolls are going to love you.

These crafty little mischief makers know exactly when to strike, often appearing just as you're about to start a task (their favourite time: after lunch . . .). With their cute brown eyes, they tempt you with seemingly valuable goods: a little excitement here, a dash of dopamine there. How about one last glance at your mobile phone before you start? A quick snack from the fridge? Some watercooler gossip? A final game of Wordly? A little TED Talk about the mind of an expert procrastinator? Come on, work will finish itself once you have allowed yourself a treat.

What do the time trolls seek in return? Nothing much . . . just a bit of your time. A minute only. Maybe two.

But beware, once you've succumbed to their terms, it's tough to turn back. Time trolls lead you down endless rabbit holes. When you finally manage to crawl out on the other side, you'll realise you have given away hours. Days, years even. And the goods the Time Trolls traded with you suddenly seem worthless. What you once believed to be jewels are now mere grains of sand slipping through

Name:	Time Troll
Scientific name:	*Tempi Trollici*
Function:	Distracting work slayers
Habitat:	Worldwide
Monstrosity level:	Moderate
Monster category:	Internal (may also manifest in colleagues)
Feeds on:	Curiosity, dopamine-lows, boredom
Approach:	Banish it
Effective Weapon:	The magic ticker

your fingers. Did I really just spend one hundred and eighty-six minutes watching cat videos?

And surprise! The work did not finish itself.

How to master them

Do not despair. Time Trolls may outnumber you, but there is hope. It comes in the form of a tiny ticker. Banish the Time Trolls with the power of the clock. Here are two spells that work wonders to protect your productivity from these time thieves. Fight for your focus with two time tickers.

But first, know your enemy. What kind of troll are you dealing with? A *defeatist* or a *distractor*?

Defeatists usually appear when you are facing an annoying, difficult or menacing chore. You still haven't sent those bills to accounting? The guys from Project X *still* haven't received your call? No need to blame yourself. Blame the defeatists. Their trick is to bad-mouth your tasks and make them look worse than they are. They sit on your head and make it feel extra heavy. They spray mind mist upon you to cloud your judgement and your sense of priorities. They cause imaginary worries and make small hills seem like humongous mountains.

The trick? Banish the little pests with a *five-minute ticker*. If you don't feel like doing your duty and the defeatist has gotten to you, tell yourself that you will only have to spend five dedicated minutes on it. Anything can be endured for five minutes, right? This way, you'll get going. And that is key. You will see: once you have banished the defeatist troll from your desk, you'll often keep working longer than the time limit you have set yourself.

Distractors, on the other hand, show up when you are about to embark on a work adventure that needs absolute focus and may even be a bit boring: fill out an Excel sheet, write a report, correct a paper, etc. Distractor trolls misplace items and seduce you with sweets and games. They'll do anything to destroy your focus and lead you astray.

When it comes to this second type of Time Trolls, use a *20-minute ticker*: set an alarm timer and vow to only work on one single task without a single distraction or detour. Twenty minutes is definitely doable, even for an inexperienced monster slayer. Stick to this spell and reward yourself with a nugget of a real break after these 20 minutes. Then set another 20-minute timer. Beware: do not ever break the sacred focus vow during these 20 minutes, or the Distractor Troll will have you as an easy prey.

Got it? Five minutes for annoying, difficult or menacing tasks. Twenty-minute intervals with short breaks in between for undertakings that require focus. And now back to work!

Origins

There are dozens of studies that show that multitasking can dramatically lower your productivity and reduce the amount of meaningful work that you can do in a day (even more than smoking marijuana, one study found, which tested participants with distracting emails). These studies show that most interruptions at work are self-caused: we tend to interrupt our work every 4 to 5 minutes ourselves and then need an additional 2 to 3 minutes to get back to where we were before the interruption. This leads to a significant loss of productive time over the course of a working day.

The 20-minutes technique was popularised by Francesco Cirillo as the *Pomodoro technique* (named after the tomato-shaped kitchen timer), in which you set a timer to focus for 20 minutes on a single task and then take a real short break.

Further reading

Cirillo, F. (2018) *The Pomodoro Technique: The Life-changing Time-Management System*. Penguin.

Goleman, D. (2014) *Focus: The Hidden Driver of Excellence*. Harper Collins.

The Sirens of Self-doubt

Silencing the sound of sabotage

'On your odyssey across the high seas of your career you will encounter many creatures. They will slow you down, claim your best people or lead you astray. And then there are those who might trick you into giving up: the Sirens of Self-doubt. They sing of failure, imperfections and hesitations. How did I resist their hypnotic sounds? I learned to be the DJ of my inner voices. I simply play the song of success to overpower the miserable music of these monstrous merfolk.'

Ulysses Kourakis
School for Neutralising Inner Critics
with Kindness (S.N.I.C.K.)

You are navigating your crew through the rough sea. Icy water splashes in your face. The mist is thicker than whale skin. The steering wheel tests the grip of your frostbitten hands. It is dangerous. It is risky. But you know what you are doing. You are a good leader to your crew – and to yourself. Steadfast and tenacious. Then, out of the blue, an eerie humming cuts through the fog. Barely audible at first. But now, you hear it clearly. Someone is singing, out there in the cold! Before you know it, ethereal voices slither down your ears. You let go of the wheel. You have no choice but to listen. A song as cold as your surroundings. 'You are not worthy. A fraud, a time thief. Go home. La la la . . . .'

And home you go.

You have encountered the Sirens of Self-doubt. Enigmatic creatures that trick you into losing hope, confidence and perseverance. They often appear when you are trying to do something important or taking on a new role, when someone pays you good money for your services or whenever you dare greatly. The Sirens' songs tell stories of past failures and mishaps. They echo long-standing doubts. They seek to weaken your resolve, destroy your enthusiasm or attack your self-confidence.

Name:	Siren of Self-doubt
Scientific name:	*Sirenae Dubitationis*
Function:	Making work slayers question their self-worth and/or capabilities
Habitat:	Ambitious and/or successful endeavours
Monstrosity level:	Moderate
Monster category:	Internal (may also manifest in colleagues)
Feeds on:	Sudden success, excessive reflection, risk-taking
Approach:	Ignore *and* acknowledge
Effective weapon:	The Mighty Melody Maker

Having listened to them for a while, you will start questioning your entire identity. You will feel insecure and pessimistic about your undertakings. The Sirens constantly belittle their victims' successes and remind them of their failures and weaknesses. They trick the work slayers into leaving the path of progress to ponder questions such as, 'Am I good enough?', 'Won't people see right through me?', 'Do I really have what it takes?', 'Is it worth the struggle?' And once the Sirens have your attention, they won't stop singing. Until your last shred of confidence has been swallowed by the sea.

Here are some of the Siren's greatest hits; surely you have heard at least one of these monster tunes before:

– *You're simply the worst*

– *Under pressure (you crack)*

– *Don't worry, be crappy*

– *We will mock you*

– *Here comes the rain*

– *What a miserable world*

– *Just stop believin'*

Through the centuries the Sirens of Self-doubt have acquired many names: the Inner Critic, Inner Judge, Super-ego or Mental Gremlin. Psychologists also use the term *impostor syndrome* to describe the condition when people doubt the value of their work without a rational reason. But whatever you want to call these eerie merfolk, you have no choice but to face their music – and to change the beat.

How to master them

Yes, some monsters are best ignored, others slayed. When it comes to the Sirens, it is a bit more complicated. They are a bit like Schrödinger's cat: you have to acknowledge them *and* you have to ignore them. For that you can use an ancient artefact called the Mighty Melody Maker. It allows you to do four things:

– **Karaoke:** Don't just sing along. Sing along in your silliest, ugliest voice. Mock the Sirens' songs with all your zest. When they go 'You are not good enough', you repeat with a high-pitched cartoon voice: 'I am not good enough. boooohooooo. I am not guuuudeeeeenufffffff. I am soooo sad now. Booohooooooooo.' The Sirens will swiftly jump back into the water. They hate being made fun of. This works for all kinds of intrusive thoughts, by the way. A little bit of mocking paralyses even the stickiest brain parasite – and allows you to get rid of it.

- **Counter-songs:** Ever heard of positive affirmations? They are short statements to encourage a positive mindset and build confidence. The classic one: I love myself. Or: I am good enough. Sounds like something a medicinal botany mountain mystic would come up with in their spare time? Probably. But psychologists were able to actually prove affirmations' health and well-being benefits. Think of it like an 'inner coach'. And make sure you sing *their* songs louder and more often than the Sirens'.

- **Ticker:** Remember how to beat the Time Trolls? With the Sirens too you can do the same. Ban them with a ticker and free yourself from their judgy voices. Tell them you need to be free for 30 minutes to write, or, say, paint, design or think. After that they can provide you with their 'valuable' criticism. Sirens are surprisingly reasonable when you simply ask them for some quiet time.

- **Engage:** And finally, you may consider taking some time, turning up the volume and really listening to the Sirens – and talking to them with kindness. For instance, use a journal to channel your inner voices. Write down what they say and what you say. A few Sirens probably just want to express their worries. Others might even have a point (maybe your presentation *is* too long and not sufficiently data-driven). And then there are those who probably just sound like your father or your mother (or both). Engage in a dialogue with these creatures of the deep. This will either take away their power or turn them into your allies.

There is a time for everything. Some should be reserved for the Sirens of Self-doubt. Some for your inner adventurer. Just not at the *same* time.

Origins

There is ample research on what is called the imposter syndrome: the feeling that many, if not most of us, occasionally have, to not be up to the job and to feel like a fake.

The causes for imposter syndrome vary: you may be overly perfect, pessimistic or dwell on past failures. You may have a social circle or a family that belittles your achievements or erodes your confidence in other ways. This is unhealthy and affects your ability to profit from the opportunities presented to you. Ultimately, it can damage your career.

So, instead, adopt a growth mindset where you stop thinking in terms of winning or losing and reframe challenges as learning opportunities to further develop yourself. This can reduce your fear of failure and shift your focus from self-doubt to curiosity.

Further reading

Dweck, S. (2006) *Mindset: The New Psychology of Success*. Random House.

Hibberd, J. (2019) *The Imposter Cure*. Aster.

The Anxiety Alien

In space, no one can hear you scream

'I first noticed its presence during a client meeting. For no apparent reason, my heart started beating fast, my chest tightened. I gasped for air. Thinking straight? Forget it. Over the years, the Alien within me grew bigger. It took charge during teaching engagements, family dinners, even while queuing up at the supermarket. Whenever the Anxiety Alien showed its hideous face, it felt like the ground had been pulled out from under me. No one believed me. Nothing helped. I became a recluse, staying home whenever possible. But luckily, the DARE-onauts came to the rescue. They showed me how to befriend my Alien – and how to turn anxiety into excitement.'

Dr Ellen Scott
Programme for Eliminating Anxiety and Cultivating
Excitement (P.E.A.C.E.)

You are at a job interview, well prepared, qualified. The interviewer seems friendlier than Tom Hanks. Your coffee actually tastes like coffee – unlike that hellish brew at your previous workplace. You *really* want this job. You *deserve* this job. Then, out of nowhere, a feeling of unease washes over you. Your chest tightens. Your heart races. Your palms turn into puddles. What on earth is this? Something you ate? Or could it possibly be . . . a *heart attack*!? And even worse, what if the interviewer notices?

Congratulations! It sounds like you are having a panic attack. Somewhere along your cosmic journey, you must have picked up a stowaway. A parasite that latched on to you during the often-traumatic trials of childhood or amid the stress of final exams. The Anxiety Alien requires time to nest and grow, feeding on suppressed thoughts, emotions and energies. Then, once it is fully grown, it wants out, no matter the cost.

Name:	Anxiety Alien
Scientific name:	*Panicus Extraterrestris*
Function:	Spread panic and anxiety
Habitat:	Space, any kind
Monstrosity level:	Medium
Monster category:	Internal (may also manifest in colleagues)
Feeds on:	Trauma, ambition, suppressed or wrongly interpreted feelings
Approach:	Befriend
Effective weapon:	The DARE Flame

   Psychologists distinguish between anxiety attacks and panic attacks. Anxiety attacks last longer. Panic attacks are stronger. But the lines are blurry. Common symptoms are fear, despair, detachedness, shortness of breath, sweating, trembling, nausea, dizziness, numbness and a feeling of going completely and utterly mad. The Anxiety Alien loves to mess with career paths, relationships or even basic job security. It does not care whether its victim is a sleepy high-school student, a stressed-out-of-his-mind McKinsey consultant, a high-stakes poker player or the president of the universe. Some first encounter it at university. Others, between the birth of their first child and the buying of their first Porsche. There are stories of famous performers who have spent years on stage and suddenly developed paralysing stage fright. Of elite students who went to the ER in the middle of the night believing their heart was about to explode. Of top managers who quit their jobs because they could no longer deal with the Alien within. They were all victims of the Anxiety Alien.

   People who have never met the Anxiety Alien often believe it to be a myth, a freakish fantasy from a sci-fi movie. Everyone who has made its acquaintance wishes nothing more than for this to be the case. But the Anxiety Alien is real. It makes life a living hell for some. For others, it is simply an annoying companion, a nasty pest in the cupboard. And then there are some – to paraphrase an old movie title – who learned to stop worrying and love their Anxiety Alien. They went on to live long, happy and successful lives.

How to master it

First, please ensure that you *are* indeed dealing with an Anxiety Alien. Have your heart checked, make sure your tight chest is not the result of acid reflux, etc. See a doctor, seek counselling and share your pain with friends and family. However, chances are you are as healthy as a vegan fitness guru after a vacation at his granny's farm. You just have to learn how to deal with that freakish thing inside you – and yes, how to befriend it.

Many psychologists suggest calming techniques such as mindfulness, slow breathing, meditation and taking long breaks, in combination with a healthy lifestyle. Our monster slayers have found all of these tools to be life-improving. But did they help in killing off their Anxiety Aliens? Quite the opposite: the more they focused on calming down and leading a mindful, healthy and stress-free life, the more powerful their parasite grew. Some of them felt they had to quit their jobs and become yoga teachers in Bali. But how did the rest manage to rid themselves of these gruesome creatures? Well. . . they didn't. They befriended it.

Picture two people on a rollercoaster descending into the abyss. One is paralysed by fear, face in agony, body tensed up. The other one goes, 'Woo-hoo!' Number two just enjoys the ride. Now, let's look at both their physiological responses. Remarkably, they are identical: heightened adrenaline levels, elevated blood pressure, increased body temperature. The only difference lies in how the two amusement park guests interpret them. One thinks they are anxious. The other is excited. Stress is what you make of it.

The trick to dealing with your Anxiety Alien is to look at it through different eyes. Do not fear the fear. Welcome it. Then, the Anxiety Alien will transform into a source of joyful energy, a creature as excited as a dog playing in the park.

The Irish psychologist Barry McDonagh devised a four-step response to do this: DARE. Whenever a feeling of anxiety, panic or despair washes over you, quickly go through the following four steps. Again and again. Do not despair; embrace the flare.

– **Step 1: D for defuse.** The Anxiety Alien loves to whisper 'what if' thoughts into your scared ears. 'What if this feeling does not stop?' 'What if I die?' 'What if my interviewer will think of me as unqualified?' Now, take these thoughts and turn them into 'so what's. 'So what, I am strong and will learn to live with it.' 'So what if I die? I've had a good life so far.' 'So what if I mess up this interview?' At first, your routine-loving mind won't believe a word you say. But again: so what?

- **Step 2: A for allow.** Accept whatever it is you are feeling. Allow it. Look at it. Learn how to be comfortable with being uncomfortable. How do your chest, throat and head feel? Which part needs your attention the most? Sometimes you may feel your muscles pulling in one direction or another. Go with it. Tell yourself, 'I accept and allow this feeling.' Over and over.
- **Step 3: R for run toward.** To break the illusion that fear is harmful, you've got to run toward it. Ask for more. Ask for *more excitement*. Say to yourself, 'I am excited by this feeling!'
- **Step 4: E for engage.** Now go back to whatever you were doing before. Engage with your audience, colleagues, interviewer or lovers.

Believe it or not, once the Anxiety Alien has boarded your spaceship you will never get rid of it again. You are stuck with it till the end. So you might as well befriend it and enjoy its company while travelling across the universe.

Origins

In academic research, workplace anxiety is defined as feelings of nervousness, uneasiness and tension about job-related issues, such as performance, time pressure or bullying. Research on workplace anxiety and its impact on mental well-being is gaining increasing attention and highlights not just the risks of anxiety at work but also its potential (motivating) benefits under certain conditions. Mostly though, existing studies have highlighted the detrimental effects of anxiety on productivity, decision making and overall job satisfaction. Organisations are recognising the importance of promoting a supportive work environment that fosters mental well-being and providing resources and trainings for employees to cope with anxiety. According to recent research this is a worthwhile endeavour. It is effective to provide programmes such as mindfulness seminars, relaxation techniques as well as trainings on emotional intelligence.

Leaders also have a role to play in this area, as they should encourage conversations about anxiety and be empathetic and attentive to the well-being of their team members, recognising the potential impact of anxiety and stress on job performance.

Further reading

Davis, L. (2023) *Anxiety: The Monster that Haunts Us Today*. University of Chicago Press.

Fitzpatrick, B. (2023) *Coping with Workplace Anxiety: Strategies for a Calmer Mind*. HarperOne.

Hayden Cheng, B. and McCarthy, J. M. (2018) 'Understanding the dark and bright sides of anxiety: A theory of workplace anxiety', *Journal of Applied Psychology, 103*(5), 537–60.

McDonagh, B. (2015) *DARE: The New Way to End Anxiety and Stop Panic Attacks Fast*. Dare People Pty, Limited.

The Bias Basilisks

Snakes on a brain

> 'Any contemporary guide to workplace monsters should definitely contain a special section on how to out-trick these tricksters of the mind. As you might know, they vary greatly in size, colour and effect, but they all have one thing in common: they exploit our lazy and medieval thinking in order to lead us away from enlightened thoughts. They tempt us into taking mental shortcuts and making stupid decisions. If it wasn't for them, I'd be sipping Piña Coladas on my yacht now. But no, now I'm toiling away keeping ungrateful youngsters from making the same mistakes I have. But hey, at least I have learned my lesson. Today, I never leave the house without a couple of potent anti-bias potion bottles. Hick!'
>
> Prof. Daniel Stickman
> Movement for Infringing Negative Distortions (M.I.N.D.)

With the basilisk, the king of all serpents, the old saying 'if looks could kill' begets a whole new meaning. Whoever looks into its eyes dies immediately. Yep. *Immediately*. No time for a little 'what have I done', let alone for your life flashing by before your eyes along with some sad piano music. Nope. One look. Bam! Your heart explodes. The end.

Luckily things are a bit different with the basilisk's distant descendants, the *Bias* Basilisks. Looking at them won't kill you. Not immediately at least. But their gaze *will* cloud your judgement and lead to stupid decisions – which again *can* lead to death, *eventually*.

The human brain is lazy. Like a muscle, it is easily depleted. It loves simplifications, patterns and taking shortcuts. Even worse: the more complicated something is, the more negatively our brain perceives it. The Bias Basilisks love to exploit this. And they are ruthless.

Let's take a closer look at three vicious variations.

Name:	Bias Basilisk
Scientific name:	*Basilisci Praejudiciorum*
Function:	Distort rational views
Habitat:	Brains
Monstrosity level:	Medium
Monster category:	Internal (may also manifest in colleagues)
Feeds on:	Ignorance, fear, misinformation, complexity
Approach:	Critical thinking
Effective weapon:	P-potions

The Confirmation Copperhead. Imagine you are giving a public speech about the benefits of renewable energies. To you, your argumentation is sound and scientific. But let's say you are preaching to a rural, conservative, elderly audience. Not one of them is likely to share your passion for saving Mother Nature and protecting biodiversity, right?

The case is clear: the Confirmation Copperheads must have had a hand in this, or at least a tail (since most snakes do not have hands). Their trick? With their hypnotic powers, they make it impossible for their victims to absorb new information objectively and rationally. Rather, they distort perception in a way that we only accept inputs that fit our existing worldviews. It's not like we do not *want* to hear things that challenge our preconceived opinions. We simply do not hear them at all. Thanks to the Confirmation Copperheads, we give much more weight to what we know already (after all, our poor brains had to work hard for it).

This is why you need to reframe and customise your message in order for the Copperheads to lose their powers and for you to win your audience. So when addressing your right-wingers, try talking about (energy) independence from foreign forces, about protecting your beautiful country from the perils of globalisation! Suddenly, you will be the one with hypnotic powers.

The Overconfidence Worms. You are planning to conquer a new market. The Scandinavians are gonna love your ice cream. Sweets for the Swedes! Who needs market research? Not you. This case is a no-brainer! Sadly, your expansion plan fails spectacularly. What happened?

A nasty parasite called the Overconfidence Worm must have slithered into your synapses and instilled them with unjustified confidence in your abilities, predictions or assessments. Whether it's your understanding of a business endeavour or a new technology, your ability to complete a complex quest, or your certainty about the future – the Overconfidence Worms will make you believe that you got this – even when you haven't. They feed your ego with fake feedback, exploit your rosy self-perception, overemphasise your past successes and wins and make you overestimate opportunities and underestimate risks – all to let you walk into the dungeons of disaster.

Some say human beings and the Overconfidence Worms are not enemies, but have been in a symbiotic relationship since the dawn of time. We have to thank them for making us take irrational risks – from embarking on a westward journey to India to inventing electric cars. After all, this made us progress. This might be true for our species as a whole. But for individuals, the Overconfidence Worms are a real danger. Again, Bias Basilisks may not kill you immediately, but eventually.

The Self-serving Caecilians. They think their job is to clean up the mess the Overconfidence Worms have left behind. They trick you into believing that your failure was just the result of bad circumstances and that you are not to blame. So what if the Swedes didn't like the sweets? It was just the weather that was too cold for ice cream. Right? Rrrright? Right.

The Self-serving Caecilians are nasty little worms that blow up your pride and keep you from taking responsibility where it is due. Adventurers who are affected by these worms are ill-equipped for their next trip: they have not learned from their journey, as they did not reflect on their own shortcomings.

How to master them

Bias Basilisks are often invisible, but don't be fooled. They are here, and they are here to stay. And worse, human progress – digitisation and global connectedness – makes for fertile ground. The more demanding and complex our mental challenges are, the more fun the Bias Basilisks have with us.

To beat the Bias Basilisks, you have to fight fire with fire. As it is known, Bias Basilisks are highly bendable and stretchable creatures. So you too have to be flexible, mentally flexible. Shamans who master the old and forgotten art of cognitive flexibility are able to freely travel through time and space applying a multitude of frames and perspectives. Thanks to that, they get to see the world for what it is – and to recognise the dangers and opportunities that the Bias Basilisks keep from us.

There are two wonderful potions that help you get started right away. While they may not guarantee victory, they can at least limit the havoc the Bias Basilisks cause.

- **The Premortem Potion:** This potion does not allow you to travel into all possible futures that are there. But it does let you see the worst of the bunch. Imagine you are working on a big project that you strongly believe in. But now you have read about those horrible Overconfidence Worms and about the Self-serving Caecilians and aren't sure. Easy peasy, just take a sip of PP1 and you will start imagining the worst that could happen. Think of it not as a post-mortem, a eulogy after the tragedy, but as a pre-mortem, a eulogy of something that has not yet happened but could happen if you are not careful. You see it clearly now: maybe the Swedes won't like the sweets. How much would that cost you? Could you afford it? What is your affordable loss? Ok then, let's do some market research after all. It certainly can't hurt, right? What's the worst that could happen? Hmm, maybe take another sip of the potion?

- **The Perspectives Potion:** With the Premortem Potion you get to travel in time. This one, however, allows you to attain spatial distance and question your position. It will boost your self-reflection abilities and help you assess your beliefs, opinions, skills and plans. When you drink this potion, you will ask yourself the following powerful de-biasing questions: What if I'm wrong? What might others think? Am I sure? Why? What are my riskiest assumptions? What am I not seeing that should be considered? What could I have done differently? What must I do differently now? Whom should I consult who has relevant experience? This last question is particularly potent. Every monster slayer needs a sidekick. And with sidekick we mean an occasional kick in your ego's side.

One last caveat in taming the bias beasts: don't drink too much of these potions. There have been stories that its smell can attract the Sirens of Self-doubt.

Origins

The study of mental shortcuts, heuristics and cognitive biases goes back many years, and has even been awarded the Nobel Prize in Economics in 2002 (for the Prospect theory). Dozens of psychological experiments have shown that our behaviour is predictably irrational in many situations. We like things to be (overly) simple and we like to feel good about ourselves and our choices; hence we sometimes make decisions that are not rational, but rather emotional, convenient and self-serving. This can be especially detrimental to our ability to screen relevant information and its subsequent evaluation. It can also affect our problem-solving ability, creativity and how we see others and interact with them. We may not even realise this, as we have bias blind spots, meaning that we believe others are more affected by such mental shortcuts than we are.

Further reading

Eppler, M. J., Muntwiler, C., Buder, F. and Unfried, M. (2023) *Debias by Design*. MCM Institute.

Kahneman, D. (2011) *Thinking Fast and Slow*. Macmillan.

Check out our very own bias.visual-literacy.org site for an interactive overview of more than 190 biases that affect your decision making.

The Craving Kraken

I want it all, and I want it now

> 'I like creatures who embrace new experiences and who
> embrace change, not like those repulsive resistant rodents,
> for instance. But the Craving Kraken overdoes it. Its insatiable
> tentacles are always craving for more: more experiences,
> more excitement, more validation and more money. But
> whenever I meet a Craving Kraken now, I remind myself of
> my priorities and swim the other way. No hugs for these
> tranquillity thugs.'
>
> Lester I. S. Moore
> The J.O.M.O. Consortium

Do not be deceived by your Craving Kraken's bright colours and
swift movements. These creatures from the depths are miserable,
insecure and full of dark poisonous ink to cloud your judgement
and sense of joy. Legend has it that the Craving Krakens were born
from the collective anxieties of humanity, a manifestation of the
ever-present fear of missing out on life's pleasures. They feed on the
constant stream of consumerist desires and unrealistic aspirations.
They are addicted to everything that promises cheap thrills, quick
satisfaction or a bit of fame and visibility. They are the embodiment
of FOMO (the fear of missing out).

The problem is, however, that once your inner Kraken has gotten
ahold of something with its greedy suction cups, it quickly loses
interest in it. In fact, it often focuses on things that are out of its
reach. Which is why you will never encounter a Kraken that is not
constantly twitching and fidgeting. The suckers are unable to keep
still to enjoy a moment of serenity or self-reflection.

As society has become increasingly connected and information
more readily available, the Krakens within grew stronger, too.
Unlike previous generations, today's specimens are growing ever
more tentacles, grabbing as many options, experiences or things as

Name:	Craving Kraken
Scientific name:	*Kraken Insatiabilis*
Function:	Making its victim insatiable
Habitat:	The lands of too many options
Monstrosity level:	High
Monster category:	Internal (may also manifest in colleagues)
Feeds on:	Greed, abundance, all things digital
Approach:	Keep at bay
Effective weapon:	The Re-now-nce Sword

humanly (or krakenly) possible. They latch on to everything that promises fulfilment, whether it's a news website, an Instagram story, a work fad or also some random committee meeting that promises a shred of influence.

They make us fall for illusions that play upon our deepest desires, fears or insecurities. Once you let them take over your life, you will be trapped in an eternal cycle of longing and dissatisfaction. Like a parasite it will feed off your energy and drain you of your happiness, gratitude and creative time. You will constantly feel that you are missing out on some great opportunity. At the same time, you will want to keep all your options open and never commit to any real endeavour – like sticking to your plans to meet up with an old friend or finishing that book you started. And by the way, never let them alone with a Yes Yeti and a bunch of Time Trolls, or you will never finish a task again ever in your whole life.

Here's a quick check to see if there is a Craving Kraken swimming in the depths of your psyche:

- Do you spend more time longing for things that you don't have than appreciating the things you have?

- Do you frequently check the whereabouts of your fellow work slayers and wonder why you're not in their cool adventure boots, kicking big-time monster butts?

- Are you envious of other work slayers' achievements, possessions or recognitions instead of focusing on your own hero's quest?

- When you have reached a goal, does it happen to you that instead of being grateful for having achieved it you immediately start thinking about the next one?

- Have you ever waited to answer a colleague who has asked you to be part of a project or an event, just to see if a better opportunity comes along in the meantime?

- Have you received gifts, treasures or magic items and then immediately wanted more rather than cherishing these newly acquired possessions?

If you have answered yes more than twice, we've got some bad news for you: you have a severe case of the squiddle-diddles. Oh yes, your skull has been Kraken-ed open.

How to master it

Don't panic, you can always quit the squid (feel free to print bumper stickers with that slogan). Here are a few helpful pointers:

– **Practice mastery.** Rather than starting all kinds of activities without finishing any of them, stick to one. Remember that appetite comes with eating. The longer you do and the more you commit to an activity the more rewarding it will become – both for your soul and your wallet.

– **Create meaning in your life.** Commit to regular activities with friends and family, invite them for a walk outside or a nice home-cooked meal (e.g. a calamari salad). Genuine deep connections with others and with nature are much healthier than the superficial touches from the Kraken's suction cups.

– **Delete as many FOMO-feeding social media apps as you can.** Immerse yourself in a book rather than the latest Netflix craze (yes, keep reading). If necessary, apply the same tool that you use to fight off the Time Trolls: a ticker! Break out of your prison cell (phone).

– **Practice mindfulness and gratitude.** Learn to focus on and appreciate one experience at a time. Buddhists say you will either miss out on everything or you will miss out on everything except for one thing. And it was the German philosopher Friedrich Nietzsche who recalled the notion of *amor fati*. Love your fate. Appreciate your here and your now rather than killing yourself over what is out of your reach. Of course, this is easier said than done. If the Kraken keeps reaching out despite all your efforts, you may want to dive deeper into the abyss and look for the root causes. Go hunt down that Kraken once and for all, perhaps with the help of a counsellor.

– **And finally find your JOMO (joy in missing out) and take the HINT (happy I'm not there).** Counteract the Craving Kraken with a Grounded Godzilla who just loves staying at home, drinking a hot cup of tea and staring at the fireplace.

Origins

The so-called FOMO phenomenon is well documented and seen as one of the signs of the current mental health crisis, particularly among teenagers, students and young adults. It is thus not surprising that this challenge of feeling stressed out because of a sense of missing out opportunities also affects the workplace.

Relevant studies about the fear of missing out have revealed the specific contexts in which this fear arises, its likely causes and remedies as well as its most severe symptoms. The latter includes negative emotions (such as sadness or regret), fatigue, stress, concentration and focus problems, sleep problems and, at times, even physical symptoms like a headache because of FOMO.

In terms of situations for FOMO, it turns out that people experience it most frequently when studying or working, and also when socialising (for example, during the weekend) with others.

In terms of causes, personality traits cannot be used to predict the experience of the fear of missing out. The degree to which one consumes social media, however, is a strong predictor for the fear of missing out. Generally speaking, the more a person is made aware of their options and opportunities at a given moment (particularly when that moment offers little freedom), the greater their fear of missing out. The best remedy against FOMO is, as mentioned earlier, an attitude of gratitude, as well as frequent, meaningful, positive interactions with others.

Further reading

Milyavskaya, M., Saffran, M., Hope, N. and Koestner, R. (2018) 'Fear of missing out: Prevalence, dynamics, and consequences of experiencing FOMO', *Motivation and Emotion*, *42*, 725–37.

Tanhan, F., Özok, H. İ. and Tayiz, V. (2022) 'Fear of missing out (FoMO): A current review', *Current Approaches in Psychiatry*, *14*(1), 74–85.

The Mighty Me Monsters

Spirit creatures of strength and resilience

> 'It is often those creatures, who are the scariest at first, that we can turn into powerful allies and friends. Find it within you to find them. If you manage to rid yourself of your shame and embrace your childlike imagination, nothing will stop you. Except the realities of life, of course.'
>
> Prof. Lady Dr Carla Young, MD, PhD, OBE, FRS
> The Embracing Archetypes Regime (E.A.R.)

Not every monster should be slain, caged, tamed, domesticated, exiled, banned, castrated, stuffed, launched into space or cross-bred so extensively that it becomes a lapdog version of itself. There are those fantastical creatures that are on *your* side, in all their might and glory. Some have been with you all along, others live in the realm of shadows, waiting for you to guide them into the light. But whether you see them or not, they are there; you better believe it. When you first meet them, they are often scared and/or scary. Just talk and listen to them, befriend and embrace them. They will make you stronger. They will help you fight those monsters that you do not need or want in your life – and they will make *you* resilient.

Of course, everyone has their own distinct creatures slumbering within (see also Chapter 4). But there are those which almost all our work warriors have encountered on their journey. So, light your torch with the *feu sacré*, climb down into your unconscious and awaken those blissful beasts. Here are few of the monster allies you should keep an eye out for.

The Purpose Pegasus. This dazzling white horse with powerful, feathered wings gives you a sense of direction like no other. Once it has allowed you to ride on its back and whiz through the air, your world becomes a whole lot bigger. The Pegasus will carry you above the clouds, into precious moments of weightlessness, where the starry night sky and the view from above will fill your heart with a sense of comprehension, control and meaning – so you can dive

Name:	Mighty Me Monsters
Scientific name:	*Monstra Potentia Ego*
Function:	Help their humans survive and thrive
Habitat:	The (collective) unconscious
Monstrosity level:	Extreme
Monster category:	Internal (hopefully also manifests in colleagues)
Feeds on:	Individuation, imagination, therapy
Approach:	Befriend
Effective weapon:	The Summoning Spell

back into the clouds and back to work with newfound motivation. Of course, each Pegasus has a different purpose in mind for you. Some are into the protection of our environment, helping others or building a legacy. Others just love to collect money, muscles or memories of sexual escapades. But – as has been scientifically proven – wherever they lead you, the purpose they give you can increase your resilience, well-being and happiness.

The Reinvention Phoenix. Humans tend to catch fire, for many reasons. They get too excited, work too much, love too much, create too much. Sometimes it is just life itself that sets you ablaze. And if you are not careful, you burn to the ground and become a pile of ash. Crisis. Depression. No way out. Your only hope: the Reinvention Phoenix, a magnificent bird with shiny red feathers, warm eyes and a golden beak full of wisdom. It teaches you to be patient, that every crisis is a chance to gather new strengths and reinvent yourself. Or as the German poet Johann Wolfgang von Goethe put it: 'So long as you have not attained it, this, "Die and become!", you will only be a gloomy guest on this dark earth.' Embrace your Reinvention Phoenix and rise again. You can rebuild yourself out of your ashes, stronger than ever before. And you can do this again and again.

The Daring Dragon. Whenever you need strength and courage – for facing a scary presentation or interview, tackling a complex problem or facing the human of either your dreams or nightmares – this is the creature that you want at your side. It will spread its wings to protect you and lend you its fiery breath and sharp claws to get what you want. But most of all it will make you *feel* powerful, which is, as you very well know, half the battle. You can summon it through a power pose, through your favourite fight song, the memory of your past successes or the faces of your loved ones, or by simply imagining this very Dragon at your side.

The inner realm of dreams and shadows harbours many other Mighty Me Monsters. The **Slumber Sprites**, for instance, remind you to rest regularly. The **Vulnerability Nymphs** dare you to embrace your tender side. The **HahaHarpies** make you (re)discover your sense of humour and face even the darkest periods of your life with a grin on your face. The **Goalgetter Griffin** challenges you to confront difficulties and conflicts with bravery and perseverance. And then there is of course the **Mighty Mooshmacker**, but you are not ready for that one yet. No one is.

How to master them

There is no need to slay these Mighty Me Monsters. Rather, summon them, talk to them, befriend and nourish them. Use your imagination to conjure your Mighty Me Monsters and let them guide you through the thicket into the light (to sign up for our cult go to www.embracethelightofthespiritcreatures.cult and enter your credit card details. Nirvana is imminent.)

Origins

Resilience (being able to deal with negative experiences) and personal strength are both topics that have been extensively studied within the strand of psychology referred to as *positive psychology*. A key concept therein for inner strength and constant self-renewal is what is called a *growth mindset* (as opposed to a fixed or win–lose mindset). With a growth mindset or attitude, we can see setbacks as development opportunities. Rather than framing setbacks as personal failures, we can view them as stepping stones on a journey to improving oneself. This requires at times a more positive and encouraging form of self-talk and visualisation. These ideas echo the theories of Carl Gustav Jung, the founder of analytical psychology. Jung's controversial work proposed that humans share a collective unconscious filled with archaic symbols and creatures. It is the responsibility of each individual to discover and engage with these inner images actively.

Beware, however, of solely focusing on positive emotions, as we will outline in the Positivity Pony chapter. Negative emotions and self-compassion can also be useful and lead us to take measures to avoid negative experiences in the future by preparing more diligently for challenges ahead. There are usually three barriers to get back up after a setback – the three infamous Ps:

- Personalisation: the belief that it's all your fault;
- Pervasiveness: the belief that the setback will negatively affect everything in your life;
- Permanence: the belief that things will never improve.

Overcoming these three fallacies will help anyone to activate their inner Phoenix.

Further reading

Dweck, C. S. (2008) *Mindset*. Ballantine Books.

Sandberg, S. and Grant, A. (2017) *Option B: Facing Adversity, Building Resilience, and Finding Joy*. Alfred A. Knopf.

Chapter 2

The monsters in others: Creepy colleague creatures

'Whoever fights monsters should see
to it that in the process he does not
become a monster.'

Friedrich Nietzsche

A Roman playwright once said: *Homo homini monstrum est*. Man is a monster to man.* Yes, we can be beastly to one another – especially at work. Which is why we must see behind the facades of suits, ties, blouses and expensive watches to recognise what we are really dealing with: an entire gallery of creepy colleague creatures. Whether it's during meetings, where you face off with Talk Titans, Multitask Medusas and Detail Devils, or in your quest to get (new) things done, where you need to weaken the Worry Werewolves, cajole the Single-Minded Cyclopes and isolate the Groupthink Goblins.

So get ready for the second term at the School of Office Monsters: The monsters in others. Strength and courage! You will need it.

---

* Often falsely passed down as 'man is a wolf to man'. But who cares about wolves really? Lovely creatures. Sensational howlers. Great team players.

The Meeting Monsters

It's a freak show

> 'It used to be a disaster. Every meeting attracted all kinds of
> monsters making it impossible to get to the point. The Talk
> Titan hijacked discussions, the Detail Devil led the group astray,
> the Multitask Medusa slowed us down and then there was the
> Dominance Dragon. I hate that guy. Luckily, I learned my lesson.
> Today, I bribe the little misfits with a nudge fudge. If they ever
> lash out, I deflect their attacks on our team's productivity with a
> lightning ro(un)d.'
>
> Holly Huddlesson
> Movement for Effective Engagement and Timely
> Sessions (M.E.E.T.S.)

What was the greatest accomplishment of the Knights of the Round
Table? Finding the Holy Grail? Beheading the Green Knight? Oh no.
It was Sir Lancelot's ability to rally a group of flamboyant, capri-
cious, absent-minded hotheads and still manage to conduct orderly,
goal-oriented meetings. Because doing so can be surprisingly hard.
If not done properly, meetings are not only a waste of resources but
also drain the energy from your organisation. They can fuel people's
confusion, anger or frustration.

One aspect of a proper meeting culture lies in recognising the
participants and handling them the right way. Here's an incomplete
list of particularly devious meeting monsters.

The Talk Titan: These verbose villains tend to monopolise meeting time. They love the sound of their own voice and believe it is
God's gift to the world. To them, meetings are platforms to shine.
But watch out: Talk Titans may sound smart at first. But when you
listen closely, you will realise they talk much, but say little. They
seem taller than they really are and, often, their contributions are
merely long-winded complaints that poison the spirits of your fellow
fatigue fighters.

Name:	Meeting Monsters
Scientific name:	*Monstra Concilii*
Function:	Mess with meetings
Habitat:	Meetings
Monstrosity level:	Medium to high
Monster category:	External (can also affect you)
Feeds on:	Badly prepared and conducted meetings
Approach:	Tame
Effective weapon:	The Lightning Ro(un)d

The Detail Devil: Let's cross the bridge when we get there? Accept the unknown? Focus on the big picture? Good luck telling that to a Detail Devil. These troubled little monsters just love nitpicking peripheral points, subtopics or other superfluous elements.* Asking one seemingly clever question after another, they often hijack the discussion, forcing everyone to go off path and get lost in a thicket of details. And in doing so, they attract another meeting monster, the. . .

The Multitask Medusa: Stop! Don't look at them! Unlike the Medusa from ancient Greece, this one won't turn you to stone. But seeing them answer emails, checking their phones or browsing the news will compel you to do the same. So unless you do not care about losing the thread and being perceived as rude, focus on the discussion at hand. The Multitask Medusa usually acts up when the meeting drags on for too long or is being dominated by the Talk Titan, Detail Devil or – speaking of domination . . .

The Dominance Dragon: This one does not care much for factual information. It is interested in power. It chooses to sit at the head of the table, interrupts others, mansplains (when it's a male specimen, which is often the case), shows off or confounds everyone with technical jargon. It moans and groans and rolls its eyes. Its body language – leaning back in the chair or spreading its legs – says: I am in charge here. Or at least: I would like to be in charge. And watch out: some Dominance Dragons are more subtle than others. They congratulate colleagues on their clothing or seek overly direct eye contact. At first, they appear charming. But do not be fooled. Dominance Dragons are a hazard. With their egocentric behaviour, they can set the entire meeting ablaze.

How to master them

First of all, chaos attracts chaos. Make sure *you* come prepared. What are your objectives? Have you prepared an agenda? Have you

---

* There is, of course, also the self-declared Archangel of the Bigger Picture. They just hate being lost in details and always ask about 'zooming out' – which can get old too.

invited the right people? Are you managing the time? Will decisions be made in the meeting? If yes, how? Who will hold people accountable? And is anyone taking notes?

But you being on your best behaviour is rarely enough. You need to set the right stage for the other participants, too. For that you can use what behavioural economists call nudges: subtle structures and techniques that guide people, often without them noticing.

For instance, choose a meeting place without seats. This will raise the energy, upend established power structures and make the meeting shorter (you can of course also just schedule shorter meetings). Or install a charging station at the entry to eliminate mobile phones, introduce a no-laptop rule or use a tracked and visible agenda.

One particularly powerful nudge to tame your various Meeting Monsters is the Lightning Ro(un)d. Ask each participant to prepare (best in writing) and deliver a short statement to address the discussed issue at the beginning of the meeting. Start on one side of the table and remind each colleague to keep their statement under a minute (if need be, use a timer). This way, you can collect diverse opinions and ideas without contaminating each other's thoughts or having one participant dominate the meeting. Particularly the introverts will feel more comfortable speaking up. Using this *tour de table* approach, as the French Work Monster Slayers call it, the Multitask Medusas must pay attention, the Talk Titans need to keep it short, the Detail Devils have no choice but to focus on the essential and the Dominance Dragons need to focus on the facts for once.

There are many other techniques like that. Keep expanding your toolbox to make the best of your gatherings and keep your monsters at bay. Because one thing is clear: conducting meetings is an art. So act like an artist. And like a conductor.

Origins

Recently an actual meeting science has emerged. Scholars have analysed, compiled and measured meeting dysfunctions and devised a wide range of solutions. The consensus is clear: we need better preparation before, more focus and equal participation during and consistent follow-up after the meetings. Many studies show the clear benefits of lightning rounds (or brainwriting sessions), compared to traditional meeting talk or brainstorming. There is also ample evidence that complaint spirals are one of the most detrimental phenomena for productive meetings at work. It thus pays to frame meeting conversations positively and use a final productivity nudge: one or several flipcharts to instantly capture to dos, suggestions, solutions, next steps and otherwise fitting ideas.

Further reading

Eppler, M. J. and Kernbach, S. (2021) *Meet up! Better Meetings Through Nudging*. Cambridge University Press.

Rogelberg, S. G. (2018) *The Surprising Science of Meetings*. Oxford University Press.

The Energy-Draining Dracula

It sucks the life blood out of you

> 'I almost succumbed to the Energy-Draining Dracula as it awaited me in a dark and lonely place. At first, it seemed charming and elegant, even sophisticated. But before I knew it, it bit me, draining me of my last bit of energy. My only chance? Cry for help. Luckily, a couple of positive peers were nearby. They saved me from becoming a drainer myself. Ever since, I have been careful not to fall victim to these forces of darkness again.'
>
> Prof. Buffy van Helsing
> The Ghoulish Antidotes and Resilience League for Insufferable Colleagues (G.A.R.L.I.C.)

Count your blessings when you meet an Energy-Draining Dracula. You need thick skin around it, or its teeth will be in your neck in no time. It drains your enthusiasm, good spirits and motivation with its toxic topics, permanent pessimism and constant complaints. Once the Energy-Draining Dracula has latched on to you, it is hard to get rid of.

As with many other workplace monsters, these creatures are difficult to spot at first. They may be walking among us in the shape of a toxic boss, an envious colleague or a fatalistic subordinate. Do you have a great idea for a strategic initiative? Don't bother; they'll say, 'Headquarters isn't interested in our opinion.' Are you proud of that project plan that you produced? 'The numbers could be better', they'll say.

Once you have spent some time with the Energy-Draining Draculas and Draculettes, their effect will creep up like an icy hand on your shoulders. To detect if you've been exposed to their negativity, ask yourself the following questions:

- Do I feel demotivated every time I speak to that person?
- Do I fear my next conversation with this person?
- While talking to this person, do I get the feeling that they do not really care about me? Are they mostly concerned with themselves?

Name:	Energy-Draining Dracula/ Draculette
Scientific name:	*Vampyrus Vires Exhaurens*
Function:	Reduce positive energy
Habitat:	Worldwide
Monstrosity level:	Moderate
Monster category:	External (can also affect you)
Feeds on:	Positive energy
Approach:	Steer clear
Effective weapon:	The Boundary Amulet

- When I approach this person with positive news, do they belittle me and try to find the negative side to what has happened?
- Is this person frequently using me and hardly ever doing anything for me?

If you have answered more than one of these questions with a 'yes', there might be a vampire in your office. So unless you don't want to roam the Earth till the end of your days in bad spirits yourself, it is time to bring out the big guns. It is time to defeat these monsters. Here is how.

How to master it

The bad news: garlic won't do the trick. The good news: there is another solution. Get ahold of the magical Boundary Amulet to shield yourself against this villain. It helps you do three things:

- **Create boundaries:** It is essential to communicate to Energy-Draining Draculas that their proximity is not welcomed. Avoid sharing personal stories with them and minimise the time you spend in their presence. You can achieve this by reducing interactions or by clearly expressing, both verbally and non-verbally, that certain conversation topics or comments are not appreciated. It is a proven fact that vampires can only enter your personal space once you have invited them in. So don't.

- **Maintain neutrality:** Energy-Draining Draculas thrive on consuming your energy, so it is crucial not to provide them with any fuel. Refrain from reacting to their comments or provocations, avoid getting involved in their conversations and steer clear of asking follow-up questions. By staying neutral, you can safeguard your energy and prevent them from draining it further.

- **Turn them:** In some rare cases, Energy-Draining Draculas have been known to be healed. To achieve this, you must convey to the drainers that their behaviour resembles that of a diva and that they need to get off their high undead horse. Utilise charm, wit and irony as your tools. Hold up a mirror to them. If they can recognise and acknowledge certain aspects of their vampire tendencies in the mirror, there is hope for change. Give them love and kindness. They will need it to transform back to their true selves.

Above all, if you have fallen victim to the bite of an Energy-Draining Dracula, be cautious not to turn into a vampire yourself. Treat yourself immediately to the *elixir of empathy* to avoid turning into a full-fledged Dracula over time. Regularly check your teeth and your behaviour towards others. Reassure yourself that you are still human and have not morphed into a walking bat.

Origins

The topic of energy at the workplace has been studied extensively in research. It is now seen as an essential element of personal productivity on par with time management or one's ability to focus.

There are two key ingredients to energy management at work. The first one consists of knowing your chronotype; that means knowing when, during a workday, you have the most energy to get difficult work done (are you, for example, a morning person or not?).

Number two consists of being aware of and avoiding energy drainers. While there may be other types of drainers – such as a heavy meal, a chronic disease or a noisy, smelly or dark workplace – people tend to be one another's biggest energy drainers. In fact, there may be people who are energy drainers for some, but not for others. A key skill in protecting one's energy is thus developing a sort of sixth sense as to who might be giving you additional energy to get difficult work done and who may be harmful to your best self. Finding ways to avoid such energy-draining people is an important skill for one's sustainable performance, success and ultimately career.

Further reading

Northrop, C. (2018) *Dodging Energy Vampires*. Hay House.

The Groupthink Goblins

Banning the collective mind

> 'These goblins can be quite agreeable, in fact too much so.
> But beware if you disagree with their dominating group
> opinion. First their aggressions are subtle, but if you hold
> on to your counter opinion, the Goblins become vicious and
> attack you with their sharp teeth and strong arms. Luckily
> there are countermeasures, but they require courage. Only
> if you are willing to risk friendships and status do you stand
> a chance to defeat the collective mind of the Groupthink
> Goblins.'
>
> Kassandra DeSantis
> League for the Encouragement and Advocacy
> of Dissent (L.E.A.D.)

Everyone in your company has been dreaming about this for years:
a product so innovative that it will change the face of the Earth.
Shareholders and employees can hardly await its launch. A bang so
big the entire industry will tremble. And you – of all people – were
granted the honour to play an integral part in its development. Wow,
to be part of your charismatic leader's inner circle! All your life you
had felt like an outsider. Now, for the first time, you have arrived.
They accepted you as one of their own. And for a while, it felt like
you were all sharing one mind, an act of creation in total harmony
and alignment. You have to be grateful, right?

Right?

Recently, you are feeling a sense of unease. You wake up in
the middle of the night. Doubt washes over you. The calcula-
tions feel off. Should you do another test round, longer and with
a larger sample? Or are you simply not used to things being
that easy?

Name:	Groupthink Goblins
Scientific name:	*Goblini Conformisti*
Function:	Defend dominating opinion
Habitat:	Groups
Monstrosity level:	Medium to high
Monster category:	External (can also affect you)
Feeds on:	Harmony, strong leadership, ambition
Approach:	Break them apart
Effective weapon:	The Scroll of Dissent

Another day, another meeting. The team's enthusiasm does not wane. Little time is left. Let's get ready for praise and fame! The boss asks if there are any questions. You pull yourself together, raise your hand. You mumble that you have been having second thoughts: Shouldn't we . . . couldn't we . . . run another test? Moans. Dubious looks. Your colleagues imitate your voice. 'Second thoughts?', 'Another test?'. Come on! One of them even calls you a Worry Werewolf. This hurts.

But then, suddenly you see it all so clearly. How could you have been so blind? Your entire team is an army of Groupthink Goblins! Greenish skin, small bodies, huge ears, the latter being nothing but echo chambers for their leader's opinions. Their sharp teeth and massive arms are mere weapons to attack dissenters. Their empty eyes eager to follow a strong charismatic leader, their necks way too short to ever stick out.

Groupthink Goblins often ridicule others, discrediting their opinions or viewpoints and defending their own opinions at all costs. They travel in packs and strive to cultivate team unison and harmony. They despise conflict or debate. They hate talking about risks, alternative options or contingencies, which of course makes them much liked but essentially horrible advisors for decision makers. They nourish feelings of invulnerability and moral superiority, even while making bad choices. They do so by emphasising what everybody agrees on, and by putting subtle (or not so subtle) pressure on dissidents so that they too start self-censoring themselves.

Before you know it, you find yourself on the street without a job and no glory, holding a carton with your office belongings in your arms. But the cactus in the box reminds you of who you truly are: an unruly and resilient creature that follows nothing but its own instinct. To hell with these Goblins and their stupid gamechanger product!

Two weeks later, you are enjoying your newly won free time in a coffeeshop, reading the newspaper and drinking an overpriced double mocha latte – which you can easily afford thanks to that golden parachute they gave you. Then you almost choke, the foam splurting through your nostrils. In the paper, there is a large picture of your ex-boss. The caption reads: 'Master of Disaster'. And then: 'The worst product launch in history. Losses and deaths piling up. Why did no one (con)test this lunacy?'

You were right all along, but the Goblins defended their territory without mercy. You take another sip and flip to the job listings. What a beautiful, non-monstrous day!

How to master them

Get ahold of an ancient artefact called the Scroll of Dissent. Depending on whether you are a leader or a team member, it offers you two different strategies.

As a leader, you must first travel within, and dare to ask yourself: are you someone who surrounds themselves with yes-sayers? Do you want your followers to shower you with praise, even if you are clearly leading them to their ruin? Or are you willing to allow dissent and conflict for the sake of the greater good, at the risk of jeopardising your own standing? If the first one is the case, you are more than likely to breed a horde of vicious Groupthink Goblins. They will probably even convince you to get a Nihmean Lion as a pet (see later).

So, make sure your fellowship is as diverse as possible and keep mixing things up. Invite the occasional Worry Werewolf, add the Oblivious Ogre, or even allow for a Single-Minded Cyclops to join your journey for a while. Create safe spaces for everyone to voice their opinions. For instance, ask them individually – and possibly anonymously – before they have a chance to hear their fellow Goblins' opinions. In this way, they will express their true beliefs instead of just repeating their leader's voice. It's almost impossible to tame the Groupthink Goblins when they are together. But you can break out of their gridlock by exploiting their loyalty: just give them clear decision or voting rules, and they will adhere to them.

As a team member, you must be more cunning. Seek allies in private conversations. Ask questions rather than confront the Goblins directly (see also the Resistance Rodents later). Underline your arguments with evidence and, if necessary, don't shy away from speaking to your boss's boss. Or even your boss's boss's boss (now read this aloud and pet the demon kitten that you have summoned).

Finally, there is one last weapon in your armoury, the scariest of them all: knowledge. If the Goblins keep disagreeing with you disagreeing, simply call them by their name. Inform them of the phenomenon to which they might have fallen victim. Send them the Wikipedia article or 20 more copies of this book. Thank you very much.

Origins

The phenomenon of groupthink has been studied in social psychology since the late 1960s when Irving Janis asked himself why smart people make stupid decisions when they gather in a room to deliberate. His findings revealed that a subtle kind of peer pressure leads to self-censoring among team members when it comes to their concerns, and thus to a pseudo consensus in many groups, especially if they have a strong, outspoken leader. This leads to the neglect of risks and better alternatives and ultimately to bad decisions.

Effective countermeasures include brainwriting instead of brainstorming, the pre-pooling of information and assessments and establishing clear and explicit decision rules. It's also important to periodically mix up groups and ensure their diversity. Cultivating psychological safety is also a good countermeasure against this form of collective rationale.

Further reading

Sunstcin, C. R. and Hastie, R. (2014) *Wiser: Getting Beyond Groupthink to Make Groups Smart*. Harvard Business Review Press.

The Single-Minded Cyclopes

Eye wide shut

> 'Beware of the Cyclopes, or one-eyed idiots as I like to call them. They are neither smart nor pretty and are often quite grumpy. They tackle complex tasks with simplistic one-dimensional solutions. This can be dealt with, but when one of their tribe gains too much power and one view becomes too dominant, your entire enterprise is endangered. So, manage the Cyclopes wisely, or poke their eyes out. The choice is yours.'
>
> Captain Steve 'Stereovision' Nuance
> The Multifacetedness, Open-Mindedness, Multiplicity of Perspectives and Multidimensional-thinking Association (M.O.M.M.A.)

Every company is full of Cyclopes. These barbaric creatures have only one eye and are therefore unable to see three dimensionally. They lack true perspective and can only ever see one side – their side – of a problem, challenge or task. You find them in almost every division of large organisations. Examples are:

– **The Efficiency Cyclops.** They only ever keep an eye – yes one eye – on lean processes, cutting costs wherever possible. Rarely does the old adage cross their mind that you have to spend money to make money. They frequently focus on creativity and try to kill it with their large fists or by smashing innovations with a cost hammer. In terms of cost awareness they are very different from the second type.

– **The Product Development Cyclops.** They are so focused on adding features to their inventions that they never leave their cave to think about their customers' true needs ('How can they *not* care about the colour of the battery?'). It never occurs to them to subtract features to make a product simpler, cheaper, more elegant or just more convenient. They are cousins of the next type.

55

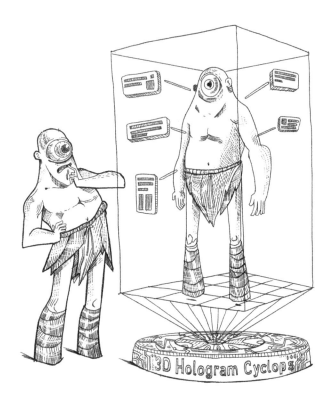

3D Hologram Cyclops

Name:	Single-Minded Cyclopes
Scientific name:	*Cyclopes Unianimi*
Function:	Inflate a singular perspective
Habitat:	Silos and divisions
Monstrosity level:	Medium to high
Monster category:	External (can also affect you)
Feeds on:	Specialisation, division of labour
Approach:	Keep tribes at bay, foster exchange
Effective weapon:	The Single-Eye 3D Glasses

- **The Expert Cyclops.** They think their expertise is all that matters. Some surgeons, for instance, care little about what happens before and after they get to do their god's work. They tend to ignore the fact that there is more than meets their eye needed for the patient to heal.

- **The Investor Relations Cyclops.** They only ever think about shareholders, turning a blind eye – again, one eye – to other groups, such as customers and employees, or to the environment. In addition, they can get a bit too focused on making the company look good in the short run, forgetting all about long-term strategy. Imagine having only one eye and then also suffering from myopia. Not a very nice outlook, right?

- **The Branding Cyclops.** They have eye(s) only for forms and colours. They want everything to look and sound alike, desiring nothing more than everyone marching to the same beat. Content? Variation? Please don't.

As is often the case with stupid creatures, Cyclopes can be aggressive. Their shortcomings make them feel weak and it takes little for them to feel threatened. When faced with perspectives unbeknownst to them, they tend to resort to technocratic lingo to mask their own insecurities and lack of empathy. When asked to collaborate, they turn into creativity crushers rather than adding and receiving valuable additional perspectives.

Real danger arises if one tribe of Cyclopes gains too much power. It will force everyone to focus on their single-minded rationality, turning the entire organisation into a mental prison. For instance, when a horde of Efficiency Cyclopes takes over, the company is likely to increase its monetary success in the short term. But soon, motivation among the staff will plummet. Lack of investments in new innovations will make it hard for the company to keep up. And the elimination of all redundancies will reduce resilience. Make sure you keep an eye – or better yet, two – out to prevent this from happening.

How to master them

Work warriors' biggest challenge is to know when to act and when to let go. Cyclopes are a natural occurrence in large organisations. With size comes division of labour. And division of labour makes it difficult for everyone to keep the big picture in mind.

As an aspiring leader, however, you have to maintain the power balance among the tribes. Actively allow for a multitude of different, even conflicting rationalities. Ensure everyone knows about these rationalities. Communicate said big picture and inform who gets to contribute how and where. It may be hard for the human brain to accept that not everything fits together. But these differences are there, whether you address them or not. In the end, this is what gives your 'system' the power to face the dynamics and uncertainties of the outside world.

Enable and foster collaboration among the different Cyclopes. Together, their world will become three dimensional. And if their minds prove too tiny to open up towards others, you can still resort to Odysseus' strategy: sedate the Cyclopes with cheap Greek wine and then poke their eyes out. One by one.

Origins

In terms of harm, the Efficiency Cyclops may cause the most detrimental effects in organisations. So let's look at their effect on innovation, and what research has revealed to be key success factors for fostering innovation in the workplace instead. Creativity research has highlighted many of the detrimental and conducive conditions for high-quality idea generation at work. A positive, safe and supportive (but also somewhat competitive) environment is helpful, as is a high ambition level and member diversity in a team. This last point fosters a diverse set of perspectives on a given issue – the antidote to Cyclopes' behaviour. It's also important to be able to develop ideas individually and in silence first before sharing them in a group, where such ideas can be further developed, challenged or combined with other insights. In this way the diversity of a team is really fully exploited without prematurely contaminating one another with the first idea that is shouted out (making one Cyclops contaminate all others in one-eyed thinking). One of the biggest barriers to creativity is the Cyclops in all of us, or what scientists call *functional fixedness*. This means seeing something as only having one function: the Internet as a store window, a paperclip as a connection device, an intern as a fetcher or the customer as a cash cow. The key enabler for creative ideas is to overcome this mono-view and reframe things and see and use them in a fresh, novel way (much like we have radically reappropriated monsters in this book).

Further reading

Eppler, M. J., Pfister, R. and Hoffmann, F. (2017) *Creability*, 2nd edition. Schäffer Poeschel.

Hinnen, A. and Hinnen, G. (2017) *Reframe It*. Murmann.

Schedler, K. and Rüegg-Stürm, J. (2014) 'Multirationality and pluralistic organisations'. In Schedler, K. and Rüegg-Stürm, J. (eds) *Multirational Management*. Palgrave Macmillan.

The Oblivious Ogre

Why ignorance isn't bliss

'The Ogre is a beast and does not always know it. It stumbles through the forest causing all kinds of damage and is not even aware of it. Most Ogres, though, just want a bit of respect, so it's good if you show them that there's more to life than their swamp. Gently show them the limits of their world, and help them expand it.'

Claire Sagebrook, PhD
Centre for Teaching Humility and Inspiring
New Knowledge (T.H.I.N.K.)

The Oblivious Ogres tend to forget who they are: not-so-smart brutes that dwell in smelly swamps. In their minds, they live in beautiful fantasy forests of wisdom and think of themselves as great experts of their craft. They are afflicted by what wizards call the 'illusion of knowledge', a phenomenon particularly prevalent among novices and dilettantes. Ogres believe they know everything about whatever it is they are doing, and love to lecture others (especially Ogres vis-à-vis Ogresses). Yet, their knowledge is – at best – a patchwork of half-truths, misconceptions and shallow understandings. Oblivious Ogres miss crucial details and, being lost in a swampy maze of ignorance, fail to grasp the complexities of the kingdom.

The main problem is that these creatures have a high incompetence compensation competence. That means, they can hide well what they do not understand, even from themselves. As a result, they intimidate others with buzz words, false analogies and confounding arguments, spreading dangerous misinformation. As a result, those who encounter 'ignogreance' often end up deeply confused and intimidated, which can paralyse entire divisions or organisations.

Name:	Oblivious Ogre
Scientific name:	*Ogri Ignaro*
Function:	Spread stupidity
Habitat:	Unfortunately, everywhere
Monstrosity level:	Medium
Monster category:	External (can also affect you)
Feeds on:	Pride, laziness
Approach:	Educate
Effective weapon:	The Dice of Knowledge

How to master it

There are two ways to tame the Oblivious Ogre, an easy and a hard one. The easy route consists of simply caging the Ogre and not letting them do any damage. That may be a waste of motivation and energy, though. Hence, the second option: educating the Ogre. Yes, it can be done. For that, it is necessary that the Ogre recognises the limits of its knowledge and that it has a long way to go. For this first step in the taming process, ask the Ogre a set of harmless questions about its supposed domain of knowledge. How does it work? What elements is it made up of? What are its uses? How is it different from similar fields? (You can use the Dice of Knowledge for that, helping you choose the right questions and engage the Ogre in a playful way.)

But tread carefully, avoid provoking the Ogre's wrath. It may lash out with its strong arms and sharp teeth. The point is to show the Ogre that there are many more elements that it may not have considered. You have got to make the Ogre find out what it doesn't know yet, and inspire in it the curiosity to dig deeper.

Origins

Our knowledge illusions have been studied in psychology for decades. Two researchers, named David Dunning and Justin Kruger, have found out that when we have limited knowledge of a domain (like when we are beginners or novices), we tend to overestimate our mastery of it. Only when we dig deeper do we realise that there's so much we still don't understand about the topic. This is related to another phenomenon described by Frank Keil and his colleagues in their studies of the *illusion of explanatory depth*. They discovered that we believe we understand complex technical devices, concepts or domains much better than we actually do. The good news is that we can be made aware of this knowledge illusion by being asked simple questions about the inner workings of such a device or domain. Our own research has shown that visualising your understanding can also make gaps in your knowledge more visible and thus raise your awareness about the limits of your understanding.

Further reading

Grant, A. (2021) *Think Again: The Power of Knowing What You Don't Know*. Penguin.

Sloman, S. and Fernbach, P. (2017) *The Knowledge Illusion*. Riverhead Books.

The Worry Werewolf

From moans to meaning

> 'No need to slay these poor creatures. They have a lot to offer – if you know how to deal with their constant howling. Sure, they tend to be paranoid, sometimes even aggressive. But underneath their furry fury, there is (usually) a rational person with valid concerns. Listen carefully, and the Werewolf might transform into an Aware-Wolf.'
>
> Joana Landis
> High Order of Werewolf Listeners (H.O.W.L.)

You may have seen a colleague transform into a Worry Werewolf right before your very eyes. It's not a pretty scene. One moment, they are friendly and supportive, the next their smile turns into a gruesome gob. Suddenly they howl with horrific sounds, and launch nos and buts at an ever-faster pace. Your first instinct may be to draw your silver sword and stab the beast – at least rhetorically. But you may want to slow down there, young Monster Hunter. There is a better way. Let the Worry Werewolf do its howling. Acquaint yourself with its ancient language, because beneath the sad sounds of its worries lies wisdom.

How to master it

Tame the Worry Werewolves by befriending them. In joint meetings, sit next to them, show no fear and take a sip from your Empathy Elixir. This way, their howling will be quiet and civil. Acknowledge it with a gentle nod or other signals that say, 'I hear you'. Now, probe their thoughts. What exactly are they worried about? Why? Are they willing to share some of their assumptions?

Table 1 Worry-Werewolfish for beginners

What the Werewolf howls	What it means for you
This will never work.	We need to figure out the process step by step.
We've tried this already.	I don't see yet how this differs from previous approaches.
Our clients won't like this.	Let's figure out how to sell this to our customers.
This will soon be out of our hands.	Others will support this as well.
That's a moonshot.	I like our ambition level here.
Corporate won't agree with this.	Let me help you with the pitch deck for our executives.
Did you check with legal?	Surely there's a way to make this compliant.
Who has already tried this?	I'm excited we're doing something new.

Questions that can help achieve this are:

– What kind of risks do you envision?

– Why are you sceptical about this?

– How could we make it work?

– Who else might object to this?

Prodding the Worry Werewolves does not come without risks, of course. They may bite you and turn you into a Worry Werewolf, too. But if you speak with kindness, they might not even remember that they were wolves.

Also, you can always let the Worry Werewolf know that there is a right place and time for everything. In a creative, divergent setting

Name:	Worry Werewolf	
Scientific name:	*Lupus Lamentis*	
Function:	Paralyse by worrying	
Habitat:	Risky endeavours	
Monstrosity level:	Medium	
Monster category:	External (can also affect you)	
Feeds on:	Enthusiasm, doubt, sense of initiative, optimism	
Approach:	Empathise with it by using its useful suggestions	
Effective weapon:	The Empathy Elixir	

you might want to ask them politely to restrain themselves and say yes for once to the most outrageously wild and positive ideas. But promise them a time and a place where you engage with them and their worries, maybe during the next full moon under the large oak tree next to the copy machine.

Origins

The concept of the Worry Werewolf was first expressed in more positive terms by the legendary, long-time CEO of Intel, Andy Grove, who referred to this as 'helpful Cassandras' – at times irritating colleagues who volunteer their warning. (In Greek mythology, Cassandra famously predicted the fall of Troy, but no one listened to her.)

When you have somebody who worries or criticises you often, Grove advises that you react consistently and constructively. Do not shut them up, otherwise you may lose an important risk detector. Turn your Werewolf into a watchdog and thus cultivate (internal) criticism.

Further reading

Grove, A. S. (1998) *Only the Paranoid Survive*. Profile Books.

The Positivity Pony

The glass is full! Not half-full. *Full*!

'I encountered many monsters in my life, Cyclopes, Goblins, Trolls, you name it. They all scared me, but this one scarred me. This freakishly happy creature kept glossing over our sorrows with its rainbow sparkles, always ignoring the writing on the wall. In the end, the whole company fell apart, with that damned Pony prancing over its ruins, singing joyful songs and telling us to stop being so neiiiigh-gative. The lesson it taught me? Believing in a glorious future is nice and all, but you have to confront your current reality in all its brutality. Because the more you look away, the more real it becomes.'

Prof. Nate 'Grumpelstiltskin' Glanzmann
The Balancing-Optimism-with-Open-and-Honest-Objectivity
Organisation (B.O.O.H.O.O.)

We meet them throughout our lives. As a child, when you fall and hurt yourself, the Positivity Pony will nicker: 'Come on, don't cry. It's nothing. It doesn't really hurt.' When your first love leaves you, the Positivity Pony will neigh, 'You deserve better anyway. Every tear you shed is a waste. Focus on the positive.' And later in life, you will find the Ponies galloping and prancing through your workplace corridors, brushing over everyone's concerns like bald people trying to cover the obvious with a few greasy strands of hair.

Here are some examples:

- You express concerns about a colleague's alleged mental illness. The Pony will say: 'We all have our crosses to bear. I am sure it's nothing.'
- You address suspicions of harassment and bullying. The Pony will say: 'That is just workplace banter.'
- You observe anxiety among the staff about the upcoming merger. The Pony will say: 'They all got to relax. Change is good. Change is natural.'

Name:	Positivity Pony
Scientific name:	*Equus Ferus Caballus Positivus*
Function:	Turn everything into roses
Habitat:	Conversations
Monstrosity level:	Low
Monster category:	External and internal
Feeds on:	Challenges, mishaps, crises, pending problems
Approach:	Help it face the facts
Effective weapon:	The De-distortion Mirror

- Your team's morale is low after losing several pitches in a row. The Pony will try to cheer everyone up and say things like, 'Stop it with the long faces, let's move on the next one!', rather than looking for the bad streak's reason.

- Or maybe you are worried about your organisation's safety standards, seeking to avoid accidents. The Pony will call you a Negativity Nancy, a Cry Baby or even a Worry Werewolf and tell you to just be grateful for once. 'Not everyone has such a cool and secure – not to say safe – job!'

Positivity Ponies are experts in dismissing worries and suppressing negative emotions. Not only are they in denial of their own reality's complexities, they also shame others for expressing their feelings and *trick* them into believing it is them who are seeing things through grey glasses. Rather than dealing with problems and addressing underlying issues, the Positivity Ponies sweep things under the rug and brush over them with mantras such as, 'Let's focus on the positive!', 'I am sure it's nothing', 'Everything happens for a reason' or 'You can't make an omelette without breaking eggs'. It is a behaviour that can have devastating effects on the psyche. Suppressing and shaming negative emotions invites anxiety, depression, burnout and isolation.

Also, Positivity Ponies love what psychologists call *minimise unpleasant messaging*, MUM for short, presenting a problem for both top-down and bottom-up communication. Positivity Ponies in leadership positions avoid informing their staff about bad news. The belief system behind it being, what you do not communicate does not exist. When it comes to bottom-up communication, Positivity Ponies hesitate when it comes to delivering bad news to their superiors, being afraid that they, the messengers, will be shot like lame horses on the track. The result in both cases is a lack of transparency, innovation and entrepreneurial resilience, putting entire organisations at risk.

How to master it

Most Positivity Ponies have learned early on to always look at the bright side. Some suffer from serious trauma and lack the tools to process their difficult feelings. They mean well, but just do not know better and are unaware of the dangerous effects their attitudes and behaviours have on others and on organisational life.

As a leader, you can try and carefully foster emotional literacy among your staff, offer trainings and address negativity openly. When you meet a true Positivity Pony, suggest counselling and be supportive. Also, create safe spaces for open communication and constructive criticism.

At the same time, you do not want to discourage vital positive energy. The goal is to find the right balance between optimism and realism, echoing the Stockdale Paradox. It is named after James Stockdale, who was a prisoner of war at the infamous 'Hanoi Hilton', where he endured torture and hunger. When asked who did not make it out alive, he answered, 'Oh, that's easy . . . the optimists'. He also emphasised the importance of faith, but warned: 'You must never confuse faith that you will prevail in the end – which you can never afford to lose – with the discipline to confront the most brutal facts of your current reality, whatever they might be.'

So whenever you meet a prancing Positivity Pony in your neigh-bourhood, saying neigh to all neigh-gativity, help it confront the brutal facts, but never break its spirit.

Origins

Researchers have discussed toxic positivity as the unhealthy tendency to suppress any negative feelings, and uncovered several negative consequences of positive thinking. In the case of toxic positivity, people block out negative emotions even in response to events which normally would evoke sadness, such as loss or hardships. When positivity is encouraged (especially through peer pressure) as a coping mechanism, this can lead to depression, less effort or loafing. Research also indicates that toxic positivity often arises from societal norms and expectations surrounding happiness and success. Social media platforms, in particular, contribute to the perpetuation of unrealistic standards, leading individuals to compare themselves unfavourably to others and feel inadequate if they do not constantly project positivity. As mentioned above, a healthy balance between positive, optimistic and negative, realistic thoughts seems to be the best way to deal with challenging circumstances.

Further reading

Dejonckheere, E. and Bastian, B. (2020) 'Perceiving social pressure not to feel negative is linked to a more negative self-concept', *Journal of Happiness Studies*, *22*, 667–79.

Dejonckheere, E., Rhee, J. J., Baguma, P. K., Barry, O., Becker, M., Bilewicz, M., . . . and Bastian, B. (2022) 'Perceiving societal pressure to be happy is linked to poor well-being, especially in happy nations', *Scientific Reports*, *12*(1), 1–14.

Oettingen, G., Mayer, D. and Portnow, S. (2016) 'Pleasure now, pain later: Positive fantasies about the future predict symptoms of depression', *Psychological Science*, *27*(3), 345–53.

The Politicoraptor

Surviving Office Politics 101

'This dinosaur has been around forever. It can move fast and rally its fellow Raptors against you. And in herds these old creatures are even deadlier. If you can, try not to wake them up – that is my advice.'

Dr Derya Demaj
The International Programme for Tiptoeing around
Organisations and Enterprises (T.I.P.T.O.E.)

The Politicoraptor is an ancient monster that lives on instinct. When threatened, it mobilises its allies and launches sneak attacks. Although not equipped with the most modern brain, it is – as its name subtly implies – politically astute. A highly perceptive creature that notices even the smallest changes in its surroundings, the Politicoraptor knows how to mobilise herds, attack without getting its claws dirty and steer clear of bigger dinosaurs. Its preferred prey are smaller creatures or those with less experience. But make no mistake: although it values loyalty and group cohesion, it does not shy away from attacking its own kind – when it is to its advantage.

The Politicoraptor is not easy to recognise. It hides underneath a friendly and well-connected persona that may even try to take you under its wings. But watch for cracks in its diplomatic facade, for tiny cues that give away its self-centred and power-oriented nature. It loves to gossip, spread rumours and drop hints, while often withholding information. It claims credit, but knows how to distance itself from failure. It chooses carefully whom to assist, often displaying opportunistic behaviour. The Politicoraptor spends its time talking, plotting, scheming, conspiring. But in terms of real work, it does not get much done due to its tiny arms.

Name:	Politicoraptor
Scientific name:	*Velociraptor Politicus*
Function:	(Ab)use power
Habitat:	Committees, boards, teams
Monstrosity level:	High
Monster category:	External
Feeds on:	Struggles, initiatives, budgets, influence
Approach:	Neutralise
Effective weapon:	The Flattering Feathers Fan

How to master it

Isolate the Politicoraptor from its herd to neutralise it. Alone, it feels less powerful and is easier to control. Remember to beware of its long and strong tail. It often keeps it concealed behind its large body, only to unleash it when you least expect it. Keep your guard up and try not to provoke the Politicoraptor without necessity. In fact, it may be better – though difficult – to befriend it. For that, use the Flattering Feathers Fan to give it praise and keep it company – also to know what it is plotting. Never, however, forget its true nature. It is a predator searching for prey. It better not be you.

Also, learn the high arts of office politics in general. Here are some dos and don'ts.

Dos:

– Build up your informal network from day one.
– Try to find out what unwritten rules govern interactions at work.
– Try to switch perspective and see office constellations from the point of view of others.
– Involve people with a lot of experience in the organisation early on in new endeavours. Integrate their suggestions into your plans and proposals.

Don'ts:

– Do not talk bad about people behind their back.
– Do not spread false information about anyone.
– Do not fight battles that are not worth fighting.
– Do not hold grudges.

Does this mean you have to become a Politicoraptor yourself? Quite the opposite. There is one creature the Politicoraptor fears more than its species mates: human beings who are good at what they do; who are smart, kind, genuine and relaxed; who have great leadership skills; who are bound to end up in positions superior to whatever middle management nest the Politicoraptor occupies. Be that person.

Origins

When young employees are asked what business school did not prepare them for, the answer often is, 'office politics'. Office politics is everything that goes beyond business and gets personal. It's about alliances, allegiance, animosities, personal pride, ego and, most of all, power. Who gets it, who keeps it, who wants it. Office politics affect careers and careers affect office politics. They can be unfair and biased against the newly arrived. If you're just joining an organisation, you do not know what its unwritten rules are, who has informal power and who has lost credit in the organisation and why. Building up such knowledge takes time and connections. Colleagues who have been in the organisation for a while, by contrast, have exactly that: they know how it works and they know everyone. And they can use that against you, if you want to make change happen that threatens them or destabilises their position. You thus need to act carefully with regard to such 'dinosaurs'. Whenever possible involve them, consult them or at least inform them and ask for feedback.

Further reading

Dillon, K. (2015) *HBR Guide to Office Politics*. Harvard Business Review Press.

The Toxic Tyrannosaurus

Bosses make the best beasts

> 'This powerful behemoth does not take any prisoners. Get out of its way and try not to confront it. Use other monsters such as the Politicoraptor to do that for you, because the Tyrannosaurus likes to lead alone and lure people into its mighty grip, only to eat them alive.'
>
> Larry Leadbetter
> The Evil Superior Containment Organisation for the
> Re-extinction of T-Rexes (E.S.C.O.R.T.)

The Toxic Tyrannosaurus is the undisputed sovereign of monsters in others. It is imposing, brash and lashes out against anyone who questions its authority. It (thinks it) knows better, does better, and defends its territory at all costs. It does not respect humans and sees them as mere figures on a chessboard. It is a mastermind tactician and cannot easily be cornered. And unlike the Politicoraptor, it does not herd easily. It is fond of itself and thinks that it is invincible. It is also very moody and may lash out for no apparent reason.

The Toxic T-Rex can be recognised by three dark traits, its power hunger, its arrogance and its ruthlessness.

Its first trait is named *Machiavellianism*. The T-Rex loves to patiently stalk its prey, waiting for the opportune moment to strike. It schemes, manipulates and bullies its way through the office jungle, leaving behind a path of chaos and destruction. The only goal: power.

Next, we have *narcissism*, represented by the T-Rex's towering arrogance and self-absorption. The T-Rex believes itself to be superior to all others, basking in its own glory and dominance over the landscape. Its every move is fuelled by a relentless desire for admiration and control. And often the Toxic T-Rex is a highly empathetic creature with a dark twist. It easily senses weakness and vulnerability, and uses it against you.

77

Name:	Toxic Tyrannosaurus
Scientific name:	*Tyrannosaurus Rex Toxicus*
Function:	(Ab)use power
Habitat:	Committees, boards, teams
Monstrosity level:	High
Monster category:	External
Feeds on:	Subordinates
Approach:	Contain or push back
Effective weapon:	The Tyrant-taming Sheepdog

Finally, there's *psychopathy*, embodied by the T-Rex's ruthless and remorseless nature. The T-Rex lacks empathy and compassion, viewing others as mere objects to be exploited or eliminated. Its actions are driven by primal instincts and a disregard for the well-being of others. Together, this so-called 'dark triad' of traits forms a formidable and fearsome predator capable of wreaking havoc and destruction in their wake. Just as the T-Rex is said to have ruled the prehistoric world with unmatched power and ferocity, individuals embodying the dark triad of traits can exert a dangerous influence over the social and psychological landscape.

How to master it

It is best to keep a safe distance from the Toxic Tyrannosaurus. Observe them, study them, maybe even learn from them. But never get too close and reveal to them how you feel. Perhaps you can make this dinosaur aware what it really is – and that it should have died with the rest of them 60 million years ago. Provocation, however, is a risky approach. It is much better to enlist the help of others to keep it in check. Summon your Tyrant-taming Sheepdog to help you herd a couple of Politicoraptors to contain and push back the Toxic Tyrannosaurus. Or perhaps you can seek the advice of a mentor in order to devise a strategy to bring down this horrifying creature once and for all.

Origins

There is unfortunately ample evidence (and research) that shows that bosses can be mean, overpowering and generally bad for their subordinates. They engage in all sorts of bad management practices, such as mobbing, exploiting or demotivating their staff.

Bosses are especially toxic if they exhibit the dark triad: they tend to be highly manipulative, self-centred and anti-social. If your boss has such tendencies, set and signal clear boundaries. Assertively protest when they cross a boundary that you find unacceptable. Otherwise document such transgressions and make your boss aware of the fact that you are doing that. If the inappropriate behaviour continues, contact your human resources department or your mentor or coach about it. Also look for other working options inside or outside the organisation.

Further reading

De Vries, M. F. (2014) 'Coaching the toxic leader', *Harvard Business Review, 92*(4), 100–9.

Milosevic, I., Maric, S. and Loncar, D. (2020) 'Defeating the toxic boss', *Journal of Leadership and Organization Studies, 27*(2), 117–37.

The Dialogue Dementors

Killers of care in conversations

'You might not see them, but they are there. In many well-intended conversations they poison the climate with their toxic breath of misunderstanding, oversensitivity, righteousness or microaggression. To resist or even slay them, you have to stay focused on the goal, keep being respectful to your mates and ask for clarification repeatedly. Then you stand a chance to dispel the Dialogue Dementors' mist of confusion.'

Lady Diana Loug
Centre for Learning and Enabling the Art of
Reasoning (C.L.E.A.R.)

The monsters we discuss in this section attack one of the most vital and crucial human activities: communication. More specifically, they poison the most exquisite form of verbal exchange: the dialogue. They sabotage it in many subtle and not-so-subtle ways. It is hard to escape them as they are powerful forces of evil, especially if you are naïve or negligent about them. They are invisible to the human eye. But you can feel the temperature drop in a room when they are present. They create an icy, eerie atmosphere of confusion, distrust, aggression and, at times, despair.

Dialogue Dementors seduce your colleagues and yourself to speak aggressively, attack peers directly and without need. They feed both insecurities and self-righteousness. With their long ears they hear the slightest shred of weakness, aggression or ambiguity, and then amplify and exploit it to create a climate of fear and paralysis. The Dementors lead dialogues down dark routes of mutual accusations and turn a probing inquiry into a blame game. They whisper into the speakers' ears and suggest complaining instead of being constructive, accusing instead of probing an issue. In this way they also make sure that you don't listen to others and that you interrupt whenever possible.

Name:	Dialogue Dementor
Scientific name:	*Demento Dialogi*
Function:	Lead dialogues astray, destroy trust and goodwill
Habitat:	Meetings, one on ones, workshops, negotiations and other conversations
Monstrosity level:	High
Monster category:	External and internal
Feeds on:	Toxic feelings (such as pride or envy)
Approach:	Cultivate empathy and follow dialogue rules
Effective weapon:	The Clarity Crystal

The Dementors' biggest weapons are thus distrust, disrespect and disbelief. They also like to use stereotypes and polarisation to drive conversations away from fruitful outcomes. We know this as some monster slayers were able to capture their sightings. Here's one fragment that survived from a team's encounter with a Dialogue Dementor. The monster slayer had to pay with his sanity to bring us this conversation recording, so read it well and use it to recognise the rise of a Dialogue Dementor in your vicinity:

Jeff: Shall we now discuss the data on our customers that Angela's team has collected and analysed?

Angela: That'd be great. I think we have a wealth of insights to share.

Daniel: Let's just hope it's not fool's gold wealth like last time you guys presented. This better be good.

Angela: Umm. Ok, well here's what we found: 86 per cent of our customers are satisfied to very satisfied with our services; 95 per cent said we met or exceeded their expectations; 83 per cent would recommend us to their colleagues.

Daniel: Of course they would, all the dissatisfied ones didn't bother to answer you. Where did you guys learn your analytics, at the Analytics Anxiety Academy? [chuckles]

Angela: Actually, we also included customers who left us in our sample and follow-ups. This is indicated in the comment here. Why don't you read before you criticise, Daniel?

Daniel: And why don't you guys check before you present? This sample is ridiculously small.

Angela: Jeff, could we do this another time when Daniel is not present?

Jeff: Daniel has a point about including more leaving clients in the analysis. Could you meet with him to discuss this?

Angela: With all due respect, Jeff, but I don't work with toxic colleagues.

Daniel: At least my poison saved us from this dodgy data disaster.

As you can see, Dialogue Dementors are powerful, shady creatures that can undermine trust and goodwill throughout an organisation. They are not, however, invincible. In fact, slaying them may be easier than you think, and Daniel could have mastered his inner Dementor. Here's how.

How to master them

To slay the Dialogue Dementors, you must know their weaponry and how they usually attack. Dialogue Dementors tend to use these five weapons of choice against which you need to protect yourself.

- **Misunderstanding:** Don't give misinterpretations a chance as they create confusion or unneeded feelings of insult. Ask the other person: what do you mean by that? That will keep the Dialogue Dementors away.

- **Oversensitivity:** Listen carefully to understand the other person's areas of hypersensitivity, and don't provoke them when it comes to these issues. Needless provocation gives the Dementors more power and will eventually derail your discussion.

- **Self-righteousness:** Try to remain radically open to alternative views and avoid any appearance of self-righteousness or arrogance.

- **Microaggression:** Every aggressive comment that could have been avoided thrills a Dialogue Dementor. Try to voice criticism, concerns, doubts or alternative opinions as questions. They are a more constructive and collaborative form of contribution and keep the Dementors at a safe distance.

- **Jumping to conclusions:** Dementors love it when we don't listen to each other, so be careful not to interrupt or mentally jump to conclusions when others talk.

But no worries. You can use the Clarity Crystal to keep the Dialogue Dementors in check:

– Try not to jump to conclusions and remain open. Suspend your judgement and approach the dialogue as a learning opportunity.

– Try to pay attention to listen carefully and extensively to the viewpoints of your peers before offering your assessment.

– Never use threats or insults in conversations.

– Articulate worries, criticism or doubts in the form of questions, and never as personal attacks.

– Clearly identify and articulate areas of agreements that have been reached and use them as a positive sign to move on in the dialogue.

Here is the conversation snippet from above again. This time Angela is actively fighting the Dialogue Dementor in Daniel. See for yourself:

Jeff: Shall we discuss the data that Angela's team has collected and analysed on our customers now?

Angela: That'd be great. I think we have some encouraging results and I'm looking forward to hearing your thoughts about them.

Daniel: Let's just hope it's not fool's gold like last time you guys presented. This better be good.

Angela: Daniel, take it easy. Our last findings were solid, as are these: 86 per cent of our customers are satisfied to very satisfied with our services; 95 per cent said we met or exceeded their expectations; 83 per cent would recommend us to their colleagues. Daniel, you look worried. Any questions?

Daniel: Yeah, I wonder: did you give any thought on non-responders or clients that have left us because they are not satisfied – and thus may not have answered this survey?

Angela: That is a key question, thanks, Daniel. We also included customers who left us in our sample and follow-ups.

Daniel: Do you reckon the sample size is representative? How did you go about motivating our former customers to respond?

Angela: We contacted 25 per cent of all leaving clients from this quarter. Five per cent of these responded and completed the survey. Do you have ideas, Daniel, on how to improve this?

Daniel: Thanks for asking. But let me ask you, do you think that this is enough? Are there ways to get more of them to participate, you think?

Jeff: Those are important questions you raise, Angela and Daniel, well done. Could you work with Angela on this?

Daniel: I'd love to if that is okay with you, Angela?

Angela: Sure, Daniel, I look forward to our collaboration.

As you can see, to fight the Dialogue Dementors we have to be firm, resolute yet empathetic towards others, and also control the Dementor inside of us to lead constructive dialogues.

Origins

One of the most important ways to expand your knowledge, to make change happen, to get things done or to solve a problem is to have an expansive dialogue, a truly open conversation with somebody. Such dialogues, however, are often at risk of failing because people may get offended or simply misconstrue what has been said. Such dialogue dysfunctionalities have been analysed extensively in research in diverse contexts such as business meetings, international negotiations, education or coaching. Among the most prominent advocates of the art of the dialogue in the organisational setting are the systems thinker Peter Senge, as well as the two dialogue gurus David Bohm and William Isaacs. What they all advocate is a mindset of radical openness and respect, as well as the suspension of judgement and aggression. For this, they recommend asking respectful and open questions and to cultivate empathetic listening as well as constructive comments. While they emphasise the open nature of dialogues, they also advocate the structuring of dialogues into distinct phases, such as context clarification, diverging, converging and outlook.

Further reading

Bohm, D. (2004) *On Dialogue*, 2nd edition. Routledge.

Isaacs, W. (2008) *Dialogue: The Art of Thinking Together*. Currency.

Chapter 3

The monsters in the organisation: Cursed corporate creatures

'Sometimes human places create inhuman monsters.'

Stephen King

You are about to graduate with a Masters in Office Monstrology. First, however, you need to finish the last module in this crazy creatures course: the monsters in organisations. They, unlike the ones from previous chapters, do not limit themselves to singular individuals. Rather, they haunt entire divisions or even companies. Some of them are enormous, permeating entire office cultures, like the Nihmean Lion. Others are ephemeral and hard to catch, like the Presentation Phantoms. And then there are those, who are sticky and seemingly impossible to get rid of, like Bob the Bureaucrazy Blob.

You must, however, learn how to slay, tame, banish, befriend or keep in check all of them to ensure a prosperous future for your workplace and your career. So let's show them what you're made of.

The Beasts of Bureaucracy

Rage against the machine

> 'Child's play is over. This is the big league of corporate colossi and business behemoths. And have no illusions, the larger your organisation becomes, the bigger THEY get. Whether it's Bob, the Bureaucrazy Blob, or Leela, the Legal Leviathan, all you can do is keep these giants in check and your armoury in order. Because they are not going anywhere.'
>
> Max Weaver
> Bureau of Organisational Simplification
> and Streamlining (B.O.S.S.)

Imagine you set out to create your own company. You start in your living room with a bunch of friends. You play Mario Kart over lunch. You are on a first-name basis with every pizza delivery person in the area. You do things differently and believe in making a difference. Growth. Investors. Media coverage. Before you know it, you are renting a vintage warehouse where your 200-plus employees enjoy a free vegan canteen and an indoor climbing centre. For the first time in your life, it feels like you are in charge.

But during a board meeting you stumble over a detail. You ask, 'Didn't we agree to focus solely on renewables?' Board member One chuckles. 'Welcome to reality,' he says. Board member Two says, 'It is not what clients want, let alone the shareholders'. They all laugh. Board member Three asks, 'Has it ever crossed your mind to step down and make room for a more experienced CEO?'

But the only question that crosses your mind is whether you have created a gigantic monster.

Organisations can develop a will of their own. Many entrepreneurs experience first-hand that at some point the system no longer works for them, but they work for the system. *L'État, c'est moi?* You wish. Rather it feels like you are now a slave of some inexplicable force. And to answer your question for you: you did not just create

Name:	Bureaucracy Beast
Scientific name:	*Bestia Bureaucratia Insana*
Function:	Complicate and delay your work
Habitat:	(Mainly large) organisations
Monstrosity level:	High
Monster category:	Institutional
Feeds on:	Red tape
Approach:	Keep in check
Effective weapon:	The Common Sense Sabre

one monster, but several. There is a whole gang of gruelling Titans that now hold *your* organisation in a firm grip. So grab your gear, young Padawan. We are going hunting.

Bob, the **Bureaucrazy Blob:** It is hard to tell what started it. Perhaps it began with the subscription for the accounting software. Or was it the hiring of your HR manager Julia? Whatever it was, it invited a tiny green drop of bureaucracy slime. And without you noticing it grew bigger and bigger and BIGGER. Today, the Bureaucrazy Blob is in control of every supporting unit south of the climbing hall. It even has a name. Bob. And Bob the Blob is what scientists call a *system sweller*. He continually adds rules, regulations, administrative layers and jobs, jobs, jobs, complicating rather than supporting growth. Oh yes, Bob puts the 'crazy' in Bureaucrazy.

The nineteenth century German sociologist Max Weber was one of the first ones to study the Blobs. He found that bureaucrats love to increase their own importance without even realising it, which results in the rise of what the anthropologist Dave Graeber later called *bullshit jobs*: 'a form of paid employment that is so completely pointless, unnecessary or pernicious that even the employee cannot justify its existence even though, as part of the conditions of employment, the employee feels obliged to pretend that this is not the case.' Just have a look at the following titles: Head of Cultural Development, Chief Growth Hacker, Group Brand Strategy Junior Manager, Engagement and Learning Consultant, Design Thinking Sprint Coach, Head of Process and Digital Development, Employee Experience Designer. Very important stuff, right?

So how do you deal with Bob the Blob? You need a Decluttering Bomb. If he wants to blow things out of proportion, so can you. But prepare for a long battle, carefully involving stakeholders, simplifying processes and implementing new technologies. And watch out, for Bob has many allies. Among others, there is his girlfriend . . .

. . . Henriette, the **Hierarchy Hydra**. Since the early days she has fuelled everyone's desire for additional management layers. Even you felt you could no longer handle more than five direct reports, didn't you? So you made sure your subordinates got their own subordinates got their own subordinates got their own subordinates got their own . . . (we stop here before – dear reader and aspiring monster hunter, you lose grip of reality) – and by doing so you fed the Hydra. Now things have become rigid. Decisions take forever to be made, let alone to exert impact. Silos are rising, collaboration is collapsing, innovation is drying out. People who were once your friends are suddenly afraid to express criticism. Morale has reached a new low. All because Henriette cannot get enough. And every time someone tries to sever one of her hierarchical heads, she regrows two in its place. Even Bob has trouble keeping up.

So forget about the axe, use a frying pan. Hit it over Henriette's many heads to make her as flat as possible. Then use the pan to cook the perfect diet for the little fatso (or should we say flatso). Feed her trust and leadership, as well as modern organisational structures, such as agility, holacracy, etc. But be careful that the cooking fumes do not lure in another monster, called . . .

. . . Scully, the **Lean Skeleton**. Though having been stripped of all his flesh and vital organs, this ghostly skeleton still moves and pretends to be alive. Once someone has allowed Scully to enter the building to slim processes and eliminate so-called waste – redundancies, feedback loops, human interaction – there is no going back. Scully has no heart, no flesh, no brain, no vitality or imagination. Only bare and clattering bones. Which is why Scully is highly unstable, inflexible and easily shattered. He is unable to learn or grow. He stumbles from one day to another, trying desperately to survive and not to lose any more of his essential elements. As he does so, he contaminates everyone around him with negative spirits, demotivation and exhaustion. Suddenly you wish for Crazy Bob and his girlfriend to make a comeback, huh? But you have better options: you can either kill Scully once and for all or slowly nourish him back to life, with good food and regular exercise. So what will it be: coffin or coffee? *Basta* or pasta? The grim reaper or the gym sweeper? Which option you choose depends on how well your lean initiative has been received by staff, where it has worked wonders and where it destroyed identification and innovation.

Then there is Leela, the **Legal Leviathan**, a monster from the deep seas. Without you realising, Leela has been swimming alongside your entrepreneur-ship from the very beginning. She has kept a watchful eye to ensure that all of your crew members uphold standards of integrity and responsibility. Her presence alone has deterred most work villains from trying anything that would have aroused suspicion. But there is a downside. Leela the law lurker stifles your team's sense of exploration and experimentation. With her long tentacles, she often attacks staffers, turning your gang of dare devils and misfits into a group of timid landlubbers.

Legal Leviathans move fast underwater and are hard to spot. They surface abruptly and can stop any ship by extending their grip and making outrageous demands, paralysing progress. The best way to deal with them? Avoidance, at all costs. Try not to do anything that irritates them or provokes them. Make sure you keep a compliant, steadfast course, as Leviathans are easily stirred by extreme manoeuvres. But once you have attracted its attention, there is no sense in fighting. It will only tire out your crew in a (mostly) hopeless battle.

So better yet, offer Leela some food and comply with her wishes. Once you have befriended her, you can even use her as a gatekeeper of secrets: she safeguards sensitive information, including intellectual property, trade secrets and proprietary data, guarding your ship against leaks or unauthorised use.

And finally there is Donald, the **Disinformation Demon**, or Triple D, as his friends would call him, if he had any. The bigger your company, the more fun he has spreading misleading narratives about corporate policies or employee performance, rumours of looming takeovers or layoffs or pseudoscientific or outdated explanations. Donald can create wildfires out of nothing, causing chaos and distrust. He loves to dominate the discourse and knows how to distort or aggrandise information. To win your trust he often starts with correct and convincing explanations and then mixes them with half-truths and blatant lies. Flapping his demonic wings, he raises dust to cloud your judgement, making you blind to the real goings-on. But don't you worry, as there is a perfect weapon in your armoury to defy the Triple D: a Megaphone. Use it to inform everyone proactively. Retaliate with the truth, loud and clear.

But one challenge remains: knowing when there actually is a demon at work. Keep your ears wide open and ask questions such as, 'Where is the information coming from?' 'Is it from a credible source?' 'Who might profit from this information?' 'Does this seem accurate, current, consistent and worded with care?' 'What does the style reveal about the quality of this information?' 'Where can I find further information?' 'Are there various credible sources that claim the same?' If you harbour doubts about any of these critical review questions, exercise caution and protect yourself from this demon and its dense fog of falsehoods.

How to master them

You are waging an eternal war. It is not in the Bureaucracy Beasts' interest to win, for it would mean the destruction of your company. Bureaucracy Beasts are everything but human and therefore not stupid enough to destroy their own habitat. They just want to have a little fun with you. A little devastating, nerve-wrecking, spirit-wrenching fun. You will, however, stand no chance of completely eradicating them. But you can manage them, and even turn them into your allies.

So keep your armoury in order, throw the occasional bureaucracy Decluttering Bomb, have your flattening frying pan ready to fight the Hierarchy Hydra, cook the occasional meal for both the Lean Skeleton and the Legal Leviathan, and keep your Megaphone close by to counter the Disinformation Demon. But most importantly, never enter the wild world of corporate madness without your Common Sense Sabre. Because, as a wise monster hunter once said, common sense is often the least common of all senses. You got this.

Origins

Academic literature on the many dysfunctionalities of organisations abounds. From Parkinson's law (work expands so as to fill the time available for its completion) to the Peter Principle (every employee tends to rise to their level of incompetence where promotion stops) many mad mechanisms of organisations have been discovered. Often well-intended initiatives lead to counterproductive results. An example of this can be at times observed in lean management initiatives. Although the practice of lean management originally comes from the domain of manufacturing, it has long been applied across organisational functions and industries. Its (sensible) main premise is that waste should be pre-emptively avoided and that an organisation's activities should be streamlined towards where it provides value to the customer. Another element of lean approaches is continuous improvement. In reality, these initiatives sometimes go too far and stifle innovation and robustness in crisis situations.

The same can be said at times for the legal functions within an organisation. But of course every organisation and every professional must respect the legal constraints and requirements imposed by its country of residence and where it does business. Legal compliance has become a significant (and costly) part of many businesses, ranging from financial services to pharma. Soon, other areas of innovation will be subject to regulation, such as artificial intelligence, telework or certain uses of social media. This can restrain innovation and slow it down dramatically. While the costs of compliance are high, the costs of noncompliance are even higher and range from penalties, lawyer fees, to criminal charges, expropriation, job bans to imprisonment. It is thus wise to cooperate with internal and external legal advisors and authorities and understand their logic, rules and regulations.

Especially with the advent of social media, disinformation has become one of the modern-day plagues. This has been made worse through the use of generative AI and its ability to create polished and persuasive texts and so-called deepfakes: fabricated videos that are almost indistinguishable from authentic ones. Disinformation is not only a problem in the public sphere, but inside organisations as well, where a lack of communication by management spurs rumours, hearsay and alternative facts. Information science distinguishes disinformation from misinformation. While the former is sent as a conscious distortion or lie, the latter is unknowingly passed on and believed to be true by the senders. Both types can be better recognised as false information if one develops a critical attitude towards information and asks the questions listed above to scrutinise their quality.

Further reading

Barclay, D. A. (2022) *Disinformation: The Nature of Facts and Lies in the Post-Truth Era*. Rowman & Littlefield.

Boyd, D. (2023) *50 Legal Concepts for Business Leaders*.

Mueller, A. and Strzelczak, S. (2014) 'Negative side effects of lean management'. In Grabot, B., Vallespir, B., Gomes, S., Bouras, A. and Kiritsis, D. (eds) *Advances in Production Management Systems. Innovative and Knowledge-Based Production Management in a Global-Local World*. APMS 2014. IFIP Advances in Information and Communication Technology, vol. 440. Springer.

Van Rooij, B. and Sokol, D. D. (eds) (2022) *The Cambridge Handbook of Compliance*. Cambridge University Press.

Womack, J. P. and Jones, D. T. (1996) *Lean Thinking: Banish Waste and Create Wealth in Your Corporation*. Free Press.

The Resistance Rodents

Gnawing off the flesh of your change endeavours

'I had much hope. We invested millions in the transformation programme. But then these foul-teethed beasts attacked everything. They made half the staff disagree with our most basic assumptions. And the other half suddenly started fighting for privileges they had never much cared for in the first place. And then, the Rodents kept spreading fear. So much fear. It was like a collective psychosis. But oh did they underestimate our most powerful weapon: communication. Take that, you filthy rat creatures!'

Dr Remy P. Piper
Programme for Energetic and Sustainable
Transformations (P.E.S.T.)

Whether it is switching from one IT system to another, merging divisions or changing the business model, for large organisations change is difficult. And the more colossal the ship, the harder it is to change course. Even when it is just by a few inches, a lot of people need to be on board. Unfortunately, every company that's bigger than a minimarket suffers from a pest plague: the Resistance Rodents. They attack everything and everybody that is trying to make a difference.

According to famed monster hunter and Harvard Emeritus John Kotter, there are four kinds of these vicious vermin:

1 **The Self-interest Rodents.** When the times are a changin', people tend to fear for their position and status. Thoughts that might cross their politically motivated minds are: 'Maybe they will take away my corner office after the merger', or: 'Arrrgh, the pivot from services to products will make my consulting skills obsolete. Now they are going to make me join the lowbrows from sales. Kill me now!'

Name:	Resistance Rodent
Scientific name:	*Rodentiae Resistentiae*
Function:	Block progress
Habitat:	Change initiatives, restructurings and reorganisations
Monstrosity level:	High
Monster category:	Institutional
Feeds on:	Inertia, stability, comfort
Approach:	Mobilise or isolate
Effective weapon:	The Flute of Clarity and Candour

2 **The I-Beg-to-Disagree Rodents.** The second monster is the intellectual one of the bunch. It assesses the situation differently than the people spearheading the change. Through its sharp teeth, it might whisper: 'No wonder the CEO went for this kind of software. She can't even code.' Or: 'What an idiotic merger. Only McKinsey could come up with such a value-destroying plan.'

3 **The No-Trust Rodents.** They follow a simple logic: when you aren't part of the leadership you don't trust the leadership. They mutter things like, 'This reeks of white-collar!' or 'Typical ivory-tower nonsense!', infecting others with negativity. The No-Trust Rodents find fertile ground in previous bad experiences and are especially dangerous if they team up with others – which they just love to do. And once their counter-movement gains momentum, it is unstoppable.

4 **The Run-For-Your-Life Rodents.** The Run-For-Your-Life Rodents are the ones that lurk deep down in the unconscious. Which is why they are the most difficult ones to reason with. Often, the prospect of change induces irrational thoughts such as: 'I will be left behind. I won't be able to keep up.' Also, human beings notoriously overvalue what they have as opposed to what they could have.

All four Resistance Rodents result from the feeling that the looming change might go hand in hand with a loss of freedom. Researchers refer to this as *reactance*. And they have found that skilled exterminators need a simple weapon named Communication. And of course they need to use it the right way.

How to master them

When it comes to winning others for an initiative that requires energy and alignment, you have to communicate your plans frequently and regularly. Make sure you emphasise both, urgency – the dangers – and the vision – the opportunity.

But in order to succeed, you need to tread carefully. The Rodents are sensible creatures. Luckily we have got just the thing for you: the

Flute of Clarity and Candour. Playing its hypnotic melodies will help you lure the Rodents out of your office and finally succeed in your transformation endeavours.

Here are the basic notes for you to learn:

- Never use threats. Just don't. Or else!

- You have to avoid expressions such as 'you have to' or 'should'. You have to!

- Emphasise aspects that will increase your target groups' autonomy and freedom. At the same time try not to highlight restraining factors. If you do that, you will fail.

- Point out the relationship between sender and receiver. You – whoever you are – and they are fighting the same battle.

- Don't categorise or use stereotypes for your target groups. There are some of you who will understand that. And some of you who will not (okay, you get the point, we will stop doing this now for the rest of the points).

- When the territory changes, your map will have to follow suit. So keep updating your information.

- Climb up and down the ladder of abstraction. Use anecdotes and stories so people can relate. But also make sure everyone is on the same page and sees the big picture.

- Try evoking empathy. Talk about the needs of the various stakeholders. Address the difficult decisions and trade-offs.

- Also, as every monster hunter's granny would say: you've got twice as many ears as mouths for a reason. So make sure you do not only talk, but also listen.

- And finally, if those infected by the Rodents' nasty reactance bites prove to be extra stubborn, you can also isolate them from the rest.

That's it. Now play that Flute like it's your very last concert and get those Restance Rodents out of town before it is too late. Or as the most famous rodent of them all, the great Speedy Gonzales, would say, *Ándale ándale!*

Origins

Research has uncovered many reasons why people resist change – from letting go of familiar routines, losing power, to giving away privileges they once enjoyed. Of these barriers perhaps the most prevalent is the fear that their freedom is going to be restricted. This phenomenon, as mentioned above, is called reactance and has been studied extensively, both in terms of what amplifies and what reduces it. The less people feel they are in control or the fewer options they are given, the greater their automatic resistance to change is going to be. If, by contrast, the benefits of the change are clearly articulated as well as many options to adapt to it, then reactance is going to be less pronounced (especially if the affected people see that they can shape the path towards such changes). Research contexts in which this phenomenon has been studied range from lifestyle and health choices, corporate initiatives, to adapting to climate change, all the way to the rise of conspiracy theories during the Covid pandemic. Some of this research has shown that people with conservative views might exhibit even stronger reactance than those with more liberal attitudes.

Further reading

Kotter, J. P. (2012) *Leading Change*. HBR Press.

Rosenberg, B. D. and Siegel, J. T. (2018) 'A 50-year review of psychological reactance theory: Do not read this article', *Motivation Science*, *4*(4), 281–300.

Sittenthaler. S., Jonas, E., Traut-Mattausch, E. and Greenberg, J. (2015) 'New directions in reactance research', *Zeitschrift für Psychologie*, *223*(4), 203–4.

The Strategy Chimera

The lion is willing, but the goat is weak

'A couple of years ago, my then-boss announced a glorious strategy: the world market would become ours! The ambitious vision was emblazoned on every door in golden letters. But did the guy act on it? Not really. The actual strategy was confusing and inconsistent, to say the least, and it felt like no one was in charge. People were eating each other alive, grappling for resources, begging for shreds of guidance. It was a war zone. Then, on a drizzly Tuesday, I got a glimpse of it in the boss's office – a horrible creature stitched together like Frankenstein's monster. Instinctively, I knew: this was the root of all evil. Never have I been more afraid. But you know, face your fears. So, I committed myself to studying the Strategy Chimeras. And finding out how to deal with them.'

Scrooge McKinsey
Programme for Leading Actions and No Nonsense (P.L.A.N.)

At some point on your perilous path through the thickets of your corporate career, a creature known as the Strategy Chimera will block your way. At first glance, you might think it's a lion. You'll be impressed by its majestic mane, in awe of its roar, afraid of its fiery breath. But once you see it from the side, you will realise that its body is that of a goat. Phew, right? Just a meagre, measly and altogether unimpressive goat. It can't do much, and it won't do much. From the side, even its roar sounds like a bleat. Unbothered, you will pass this strange creature and continue your journey. But watch out, for the Strategy Chimera has the tail of a serpent. Unlike the head, this body part of the Strategy Chimera is dangerous. And it will attack you when you least expect it, especially when you turn your back on it.

Name:	Strategy Chimera
Scientific name:	*Chimaera Strategiae*
Function:	Assemble inconsistent business strategies
Habitat:	Board rooms
Monstrosity level:	High
Monster category:	External
Feeds on:	Power, ambition, overconfidence, optimism
Approach:	Dissect and reassemble
Effective weapon:	The Reflection Cage

The Strategy Chimera is a frequent apparition in large organisations. It shows up whenever leaders – or people who see themselves as such – come up with grand strategic visions without having the power(s), skills, tenacity, resources and political finesse to follow suit. It can also be the result of simply inconsistent elements and unresolved trade-offs. Let us have a closer look at its parts.

The head is that of a fire-breathing lion. It is courageous and proud and sets ambitious goals. Let's become market leader! Let's conquer Scandinavia! Let's turn our local shop chain into a global conglomerate. The underlying belief system: words create reality. Once you make yourself a lovely vision board, things will manifest themselves as if by magic. But if only the flesh was as willing as the spirit. Because the Strategy Chimera has . . .

. . . **the slow body of a goat**, a good-natured animal that likes to take it easy. It is difficult to mobilise and prefers regurgitating leaves over digesting powerful proteins (the chimeras' diet has been the subject of extensive studies but remains a mystery). The lion's head may have big ambitions of where it wants to go, yet it often forgets about its body, which is slow and can stumble over its own hooves.

Strategic words need to be followed by well-aligned and well-guided actions. Aspiration is nice and all, but do we have the budget? Did we allocate resources to the strategic pillars and priorities? Do we even have pillars and priorities? Can we break them down into detailed measures? Who is in charge? Will the goat walk the lion's talk? And will they be able to control the . . .

. . . **sneaky serpent's tail?** Because this last part of the Strategy Chimera has a strong will of its own. It is opportunistic and hard to control. Often it is the one that wags the head and body. It is a political creature that exploits strategies for its own ambitions. Think of middle managers trying to position themselves by use of ambitious slide decks, or of silos competing for budgets and attention rather than helping each other out.

The intrusion of a Strategy Chimera can have a paralysing, or even lethal, effect on an organisation. Its roaring head can lead to a quick uptick in motivation and positive energy, only to leave behind a hole of disillusionment. Its weak body may drain the company of resources that it desperately needs elsewhere. The serpent's tail often fuels existing office politics (see also the chapter on the Politicoraptor). The three elements combined can turn an entire corporation into a messy Moloch that is caught up in internal conflicts, frequent missteps and that suffers an identity crisis.

As if the normal Strategy Chimera wasn't nuisance enough, there is one mutation that has an even stronger paralysing effect on organisations: The Double-headed Strategy Chimera. This variation has not one but two heads. And most of the time they have aspirations that do not go well together. One of them wants the cake, the other wants to eat it (which may direct office monster scientists towards more promising answers regarding the aforementioned question regarding the Chimera's preferred diet).

A famous example is, 'Let's create the cheapest and the most beloved solution in the world.' Here, one of the lion heads seems to be aiming for cost leadership, that is, the cheapest solution. The other one appears to believe differentiation is the way to go, that is, the most beloved solution. But, as God of Strategy and Harvard Emeritus Michael Porter has pointed out: the two rarely make for a good match. It is the companies whose strategies focus on either cost leadership or differentiation that have the best chances to make it big. For instance, Dell focused on cheap computers, Apple on great ones. Because in the end, strategy is about choosing not only what to do, but also what not to do.

How to master it

When a Strategy Chimera is wreaking havoc, your options are limited. You can deal with it and try to contain the damage. Or you can kill it and then breed a new Strategy Creature.

Option 1: the Frankenstein. Grab a scalpel, some clamps, thread and needle and get to work. Shave off the lion's mane, sew up its fire glands and turn its megalomaniacal ambitions into realistic aspirations. If you are dealing with two heads, you have no choice but to amputate one of them. Throw it into a large glass jar of formaldehyde and save it for later. Now transplant some muscles into the neck and body. Inject implementation steroids if necessary. As for the tail: feed it with a couple of Mediation Mice, tie a knot in it and do not get bitten. If you are lucky, your patient won't die on the operating table. If it survives, you now have a strategy that might get you through the next couple of months or even years, not exactly pleasing but perhaps appeasing your shareholders and employees. If it does, see Option 2.

Option 2: the Bellerophon. How did the Greek hero Bellerophon deal with the original chimera? He jumped on his flying horse, attacked from above and shot a lead arrow into the creature's mouth. The lion's fiery mouth melted the lead, which then flowed down its throat and poisoned its goaty organs. You don't have to be as cunning. Just throw the Chimera – usually in the form of a slide deck – out of your window and then start from scratch. Create a Strategy Creature where head, body and tail fit together. A dragon maybe? A majestic oliphant? Or perhaps a three-legged chicken? All is well, as long as vision, mission and aspiration are anchored in reality, there is evidence to support your hypotheses, your measures and priorities are well categorised (and financially supported), and there is a group of monster riders able and willing to guide your new Strategy Creature towards its destiny.

Whatever you end up doing, do as any good monster hunter would: find yourself an interesting specimen, maybe even a double-headed one, lock it up in a reflection cage and study it up close. (Maybe you'll even find out what it likes to eat.)

Origins

Strategic goals should mutually reinforce each other if a strategy is to succeed – ideally. Strategising means deciding what not to do and what not to be, according to one of strategy's foremost thinkers, Michael Porter. Being everything to everyone is the same as not having a strategy. And an organisation is likely to burn out if management asks it to be too many things at once, or pursue goals that are mutually inconsistent.

Strategists must thus pay careful attention to trade-offs and combine strategic goals judiciously. When considering such trade-offs, it makes sense to be explicit and weigh objectives: how much of one strategic goal are you willing to sacrifice to achieve another? For example, how much short-term profit are you willing to give up to finance your future growth? How much can you delay your product launch to improve its ecological profile? Being clear about such trade-offs helps the entire organisation recognise strategic trade-offs and deal with Strategy Chimeras that are already in the wild.

Further reading

Porter, M. (1996) 'What is strategy?', *Harvard Business Review*. November–December Edition.

Seidler, M., Mehling, F. and von Nitzsch, R. (2022) 'How to make strategic trade-offs', *Harvard Business Review*.

The Project Zombie

How to end things once and for all

> 'Did we think we had finished it? Yes. Were we overly
> confident? Perhaps. Was it foolish to turn our backs on it,
> allowing this creature to come back from the dead and gnaw
> the flesh off my two best warriors? Absolutely. The lesson?
> Whenever you end a project, make sure it's dead. Chop it up
> real good. Seriously, you don't want loose ends to sneak up
> on you when you least expect it.'
>
> Arnold 'Zombie Zapper' Schaefer
> Projects Abandoned and Cancelled for Kill (P.A.C.K.)

Every project has a lifespan. Whether you are implementing new
software to manage your client relationships, restructuring your
life sciences division or planning a cool product collaboration with
a consumer brand, you ideate, plan, negotiate, allocate, implement,
adjust and, at some point, you bring it to an end. This means you
either cross the finish line or – to stay within the same metaphor –
you use your last bit of breath to whimper a pathetic 'abort' and then
drag yourself to the pub next to the race track to drown your sorrows. You do either or.

Unless you want to create a Project Zombie – or as some monster
hunters from afar call it: a Zombie Project. Maybe the client relationship software was installed and the project officially ended,
but it then turned out to be flawed. This led to costly follow-ups
and errors, absorbed hours of everyone's time and tested the entire
organisation's frustration tolerance. Or perhaps you are still waiting
for a decision to be made on the product collab. It has been seven
months since the last milestone, and you are still writing back and
forth, stringing everyone along. Come on, it is such a cool project!
It just *has* to happen. But deep down you know: it is *not* going to.
Pull the plug, let it die a natural death and focus on more promising
opportunities.

Name:	Project Zombie
Scientific name:	*Zombia Projectae*
Function:	Haunting people by coming back from the grave
Habitat:	Innovation projects, software projects, infrastructure projects
Monstrosity level:	High
Monster category:	Institutional
Feeds on:	Unfinished business, sloppiness
Approach:	Proper closure
Effective weapon:	The Debriefing Ritual

When they were among the living, Project Zombies often were the ones everyone loved. But somewhere along the way, they turned into monsters, haunting the corridors of both your office and your mind, causing pain and grievance. They use up resources, block processes and infect healthy current projects.

Luckily, our hunters captured a couple of those diverse and horrifying creatures. We locked them up and studied them from up close, ignoring their moans and spits – so you don't have to. What have we found? Zombies are humanmade. And it seems like the infection usually came from a combination of unfortunate events:

- The project had more far-reaching implications than people realised – or were willing to realise.
- No one allocated resources that allowed for a seamless integration into line management or other day-to-day operations.
- Nobody took care of adequate project documentation.
- And no one addressed loose ends or unfinished tasks.

Project Zombies can also arise from what behavioural economists call an *escalation of commitment* or the sunk cost fallacy. This term describes our tendency to invest more resources into a struggling or lagging project even though the chances of it becoming a success are sinking by the day. People will say: 'We've invested so much already. We've come so far', only to throw more time and money into the bottomless pit.

At times, even an entire organisation can become the living dead. Zombie viruses seem to be particularly attracted by the fresh blood of younglings. The so-called 'Living dead startup' is a company that is still in operation but struggling to grow or remain relevant in the market. It is in a state of limbo, with founders and employees uncertain what to do. Often they cling on to the illusion that the 'hockey stick' – a sudden surge in growth – is just around the corner. Their baby is too good to leave. But it is also too bad to stay. So they nurture the zombie instead of finishing it off.

How to master it

Forget about headshots, decapitation or vaccination when it comes to Project Zombies. But there is a way to prevent or contain Project Zombie outbreaks, if you are willing to put in the work and to take tough decisions.

Of course, it is best to avoid the Zombie plague altogether. Emphasise proper project closure, thorough documentation and proactive communication with stakeholders. Actively monitor and address lingering issues. This is especially important for software-related initiatives. To spot a Project Zombie and contain it, ask your project team the following questions at the end of every project:

- Did we close all contracts?
- Have we reassigned the involved staff?
- Have we informed everyone who will be affected by the project outcomes?
- Is the project documentation complete, understandable and readily accessible?
- Is there a clear follow-up with accountabilities regarding the 'after life' of the project?
- And did we officially declare the project completed or cancelled?

It does not matter what kind of project you are dealing with. It may be a success, having reached a ripe age and now ready to pass on naturally. Or, it may have fallen ill in its middle age, compelling you to pull the plug. In any case, make sure you give your projects a proper, ritualistic burial. Otherwise, it will likely roam your offices, stuck between the land of the living and the realm of the dead.

If this happens, you must identify potential escape or attack routes. What current projects or ongoing activities are in danger of becoming infected? Inform the people involved in those. When it comes to this work monster, it's better to be paranoid than sorry. Fathom worst case scenarios how the Zombies might wreak havoc.

In severe cases assemble a special task force to contain the out-break. Otherwise, to paraphrase a famous zombie film, the end might be extremely freaking nigh.

Origins

Unintended consequences of completed projects have been studied and documented in the relevant project management literature, but not extensively so. The technical term used for such a Project Zombie is a *lingering* or *failed project*. But even successfully completed projects may come back as undead when their unintended side effects become visible. This can be the case not only with IT projects, but also with legal, compliance or regulatory projects which may create constraints that cause friction later on in other endeavours. Other project types that may come back to haunt an organisation are outsourcing projects (where important knowledge may be lost) or other external cooperation projects. It is thus vital to pay attention to a proper project closure that includes assigning accountability to deal with follow-up issues involving the project. Such questions have been addressed extensively in what is called project postmortems, project debriefings or project lessons learned. One of the co-authors of this book (Martin) has even compiled the most essential techniques to close the project coffins in the best way possible (see the following reference) so that the Zombies can never come back.

Further reading

Larson, E. W. and Gray, C. F. (2011) *Project Management. The Managerial Process*. McGraw-Hill. (This one even contains a ghost story as a case study on p. 563.)

Schindler, M. and Eppler, M. J. (2003) 'Harvesting project knowledge: A review of project learning methods and success factors', *International Journal of Project Management, 21*, 219–28.

The Fad Fairies

Enchant me first, annoy me later

'Ah the buzzing Fad Fairies. Back in the day, when I was
hopping from one staff position to another, I was dying to
collect them all. Adopting all those cool new management
trends made me feel creative, alive, important. My inner child
could not have been happier – at first. After a while, disillusion
kicked in and the Fairies' noise became a nuisance. Very few
of the concepts that I tried to bring into the workplace had
a lasting effect. People started to be annoyed, 'What's the
Fad of the Week?' they asked. I had no choice but to become
more critical and selective in my fairy company. Also I found
meaning elsewhere. Have you read my children's book? It's
about a group of pixies trying to save the world from dullness.'

Petra Pen
National Organisation for the Fight Against
Daftness (N.O.F.A.D.)

Not too long ago most corporate kingdoms were cubicle farms.
Workers toiled away in tiny boxes, shielded from distractions. They
were cogs in a machine, leading a monotonous existence. But with
the rise of digital technologies, efficiency ceased to be the prime
directive. The rulers of the new world demanded their vassals to
'think different', be creative and collaborate across hierarchies
and functions. As a result they tore down walls and created what
became known as the open plan office. Now everyone got to roam
freely through the organisation, talk to everyone, exchange ideas
and have no physical obstacles when it came to bringing these ideas
to life. And what seemed to make sense for Silicon Valley soon
conquered the rest of the business world. Insurance companies
and banks wanted to be just as hip and modern. At first, everyone
was thrilled. Collaboration! Creativity! Freedom! But within a few
years, the craze fizzled out. Not surprisingly, people suffered from a
lack of concentration and focus. Leaders were surprised by the drop
in efficiency. And soon, walls rose again.

Name:	Fad Fairy
Scientific name:	*Pixides Novitates Gubernationis*
Function:	Distract with latest trends
Habitat:	Management meetings, strategy sessions, staff positions
Monstrosity level:	Medium
Monster category:	Institutional
Feeds on:	Collectivism, followership, pseudo innovation
Approach:	Dissect and reassemble
Effective weapon:	The Tiny Wingcutter Scissors

The open plan office is a typical example of the Fad Fairies plague. They are pixie-like creatures that love to enchant their victims with seemingly grand ideas and buzzwords, only to leave them disillusioned, annoyed and with lots of money spent. Often the Fairies start off with quite clever and substantiated concepts, which are then dumbed down during long journeys through business schools, conferences, back offices, YouTube videos, consultancies or business books (unlike the one you are holding in your hands of course).

Most recently, the Fairies have infected organisations with the idea that hierarchies and structures are useless (Agility!), key performance indicators are a thing of the past and should be replaced by pretty much the same thing (OKRs!), that new products can be developed in a standardised yet fun process that makes everyone feel like a character from *The Lord of the Rings* (Design Thinking!) and that the blockchain – whatever it is – will turn us all into billionaires. Once the Fad Fairies find a catchy idea, they will not stop until even the last mom and pop store at the end of the world has tried to implement it.

But not every idea is equally contagious, infectious and idiotic. For a concept to become a management fad, it has to meet certain criteria. So, whenever a consultant, a business school professor, a tech guru or a colleague informs you about a great new model, approach or framework, consider the following questions:

– Promise: Does the framework promise to radically revolutionise your business – or parts of it?

– One size fits all: Is it applicable to a wide range of areas, even yours?

– Simplicity: Is it simple enough to fit into a catchy acronym, a four-sections matrix or an iceberg metaphor?

– Hipness: Have cool people and cool companies and cool industries been using it all along? And have they been telling everyone how frEaKinG cOoL it is?

So if the idea or the concept is too P.O.S.H. for its own good, chances are that the Fad Fairies are behind it.* Here is how to protect yourself against their hypnotic magic.

How to master them

The Fad Fairies aren't as toxic as the Energy-Draining Dracula or as fatal as the Strategy Chimera. Obviously, experimentation and excitement for new models and frameworks are necessary for successful and fun-to-work-for organisations. Most Fad Fairies – including the aforementioned ones – bring you *some* valuable elements. But it is important to face the Fairies with a healthy dose of scepticism. If you blindly accept and apply every new TED Talk model, you might end up not only wasting a lot of money, energy and focus, but also losing your colleagues' trust.

Here are four guiding principles that help you deal with those enchanting little mischief makers:

1 **True North:** Some companies and departments are more prone to fall victim to the Fad Fairies than others. Think of it as a religious cult. People who lack purpose and (self-)leadership are more likely to end up in a sect conversion centre. Make sure both your organisation and everyone in it has a clear sense of purpose, belonging, vision and urgency. Otherwise they will look elsewhere. This is especially the case for everyone not directly involved in the daily business. Bureaucrats love nothing more than inflating their own importance. And the Fad Fairies just love to be of assistance there (see also, the Bureaucracy Beasts).

2 **Timing:** Take advantage of others' mistakes. Pioneers and explorers are the most likely ones to be killed by wild animals and such. If there is a new appealing management trend, then wait for others to implement it first. What has worked? What hasn't? What will eventually blow over and what will last?

---

* This should of course be a management fad itself: 'the P.O.S.H method. How to resist the cult of management trends and make up your own mind'. Soon to be a major Ted Talk, Hollywood franchise and religious movement.

3 **Selectivity:** Too many Fad Fairies can drown out initiatives that are of actual importance and necessity. It is the old cautionary tale of the boy who cried wolf: If you bombard your colleagues with too much novelty too often, they might stop listening to you when it really matters. Select carefully what new concepts you want your organisation to absorb. Only select those parts that cater to your needs, and then don't shy away from adapting them to the needs and context of your organisation (and its culture and heritage).

4 **Dialectics:** Think like Hegel, the German philosopher: thesis, antithesis, synthesis. The new enhances, complements and changes the old. It never just replaces it. And it certainly is not automatically better. The concept of Agility should not turn the entire organisation into a spineless jellyfish, but add a certain amount of flexibility and speed to an otherwise stable organism. The idea of the open plan office is not supposed to create one big concert venue, but change the floor plan in a way so it allows to cater to both efficiency and innovation.

Hence watch out: The Fad Fairies can create a buzz about everything. But sometimes it is just a fuss about nothing. Not always, but sometimes. So know when to cut off their wings, and when to let them fly.

Origins

Management fads are as old as management itself, and academics have researched the phenomenon extensively, dedicating entire special issues of journals to the topic. Prime examples of such management fashions are the Total Quality Management movement, the Business Process Reengineering approach, the Knowledge Management idea or the use of Design Thinking for innovation efforts.

Scholars explain these phenomena through the actors that most profit from them, such as management consultants and their extensive networks, business schools or business book publishers. But seeing management fads only as a business falls short of their potential benefits to focus collective attention, mobilise creativity or tackle long-standing issues.

Researchers have examined the rhetoric with which such trends are launched and legitimised and contrast them with the often-harsh implementation reality. In corporate life, there is often only a vague similarity between what is adopted from the general framework of the fashion and the core idea of the new movement. In fact, managers and professionals may appropriate a fashionable term simply to sell what they are already working on to decision makers (i.e. the intranet relaunch is suddenly rebranded as a knowledge portal).

Another problematic aspect of management fads, that is often examined in the relevant literature, is the tendency to repackage old ideas and give them new labels. This is also due to the fact that many management fads don't have staying power and recede to the background of corporate attention within a few years.

Management fashions, from a scholarly point of view, are thus a highly ambiguous phenomenon. While they may have merit to introduce novel ideas and perspectives into organisations and synchronise joint action on long-standing issues, they often fail to deliver on their promise or are enacted quite differently than intended by their proponents.

Further reading

Gibson, J. and Tesone, D. V. (2001) 'Management fads: Emergence, evolution, and implications for managers', *The Academy of Management Executive*, *15*(4), 122–33.

Miller, D. and Hartwick, J. (2002) 'Spotting management fads', *Harvard Business Review*. October Edition. https://hbr.org/2002/10/spotting-management-fads

Newell, S., Robertson, M. and Swan, J. (2001) 'Management fads and fashions', *Organization*, *8*(1), 5–15.

The Nihmean Lion

You shall not pass

> 'The Nihmean Lion's mane is impenetrable and its pride
> without compare. Once it blocks the gateway to your
> company's holy cave of creativity, there is no chance for
> outside ideas and inventions to enter. But do not despair, as
> there is often a second entrance. Sneak up to this fearsome
> creature from behind and ~~strangle it with all your might~~
> invite it for a dance.'
>
> Prof. Alexandra Van Tastic
> Cooperative for the Open Mental Embrace
> of Innovations (C.O.M.E.-I.N.)

Have you heard of the Nemean Lion, the proud and fearsome monster
from ancient Greece known for its impenetrable golden fur and sharp
claws? It took no lesser hero than the legendary Hercules to defeat it.
At first, he tried it the conventional way: arrows, spears, swords. But
none of his usual weapons worked. Hercules soon realised he needed
a mix of wit and human strength. Clever as he was, he blocked one
of the two entrances to the lion's cave and entered through the other,
attacking the lion from behind, strangling it with his bare hands.

Now, what only the most widely travelled monster hunters are
aware of is that the Nemean Lion has a direct descendant that roams
research institutes, think tanks, corporations and startups: the
Nihmean Lion. Its first three letters stand for *not invented here* and
the 'mean' stands for . . . well, mean.

Unlike the original Nemean Lion who was just chilling in his cave,
making tzatziki out of wanna-be heroes, its great-great-great-great-
great-(for paper-saving reasons we are saving ourselves a couple
of greats)-great-grandchild harbours far bigger aspirations. It sees
itself as the ultimate innovator, a combination of Nikola Tesla and
Leonardo da Vinci, except with an even nicer mane. The Nihmean
Lion is so proud of its own ideas that it does not accept anything that
was not conjured up by itself and/or its team. It dismisses solutions

Name:	Nihmean Lion
Scientific name:	*Panthera Leo Egocentricus*
Function:	Fend off innovations from elsewhere
Habitat:	Research and development teams, product development teams, innovation teams
Monstrosity level:	Medium
Monster category:	Institutional
Feeds on:	Professional pride, success, isolation, envy
Approach:	Dissect and reassemble
Effective weapon:	The Trident of Creativity

from the outside world and comes up with all kinds of defences against them. Nothing must get past its shiny fur. And since it has won so many fights in the past, it suffers from an illusion of omniscience, invulnerability and mastery.

The Nihmean Lion loves to transform innovative open spaces into closed(-minded) caves. Whether it is a research and development department, a marketing agency or a design thinking playground: when the Nihmean Lion takes ahold of things, people will stop looking at others' ideas, papers and concepts – which can lead entire organisations to their demise. Rumour has it, the managers at Blackberry, a smartphone company, laughed when the iPhone came out. The video rental chain Blockbuster was offered to buy Netflix, but didn't see the value in it. One of the core beliefs behind their rationale: what we did not conceive ourselves is worthless.

How to master it

Innovators who fall prey to the Nihmean Lion often fear losing control, lack the time and energy for opening up to others, and live in an ego-driven culture of pressure, power games and very little trust. Also, the Nihmean Lion has a symbiotic relationship with the Confirmation Copperhead (see Bias Basilisks) and lives off humanity's tendency to underestimate the value of external information.

So, what doors do you have to block and which ones do you have to leave wide open so that your (inner) hero can defeat this outdated creature?

We suggest you use the Trident of Creativity:

First, culture. Foster a culture of open innovation, diversity and cross-functionality. Reward collaboration across silos. Allow people to take their time to go outside of their usual habitat and develop formal processes for evaluating external ideas and bringing them inside your organisation.

Second, Ikea. Sometimes, a Greek problem needs a Swedish solution. The Ikea trick is about pitching, presenting or offering half-finished things – for example, a disassembled shelf called Högadal – and then inviting your target group to finish it themselves. This raises their sense of ownership and pride and therefore your chance to get what you want. Because what you finish or put together yourself is dearer to you. That is called in psychology the *Ikea effect*. So, involve the lion early on when adopting a solution that you bring in from the outside world and this to a point that it almost becomes his own invention. Suggest something new merely as a starting point for his ingenuity. Instead of strangling the lion, invite it for a dance.

Finally and always, education. Address the Nihmean Lion in the room. Once people know its name, they might be able to penetrate its mane.

Origins

The not-invented-here syndrome has been observed in many organisations and industries. It's a main barrier for the adoption of innovations inside an organisation and expresses itself through a myriad of often fake arguments. In a nutshell, the not-invented-here syndrome refers to a negative attitude of employees against externally developed knowledge, but it can also arise when an innovation stems from another department within the same organisation. It can even arise when customers suggest product improvements to an organisation or if governments make novel, well-justified demands from corporations. The root cause of the problem lies in a wrong kind of professional pride and a premature dismissal of others' capabilities. While the not-invented-here syndrome is mostly discussed as an organisational phenomenon, you can also apply this to your very own behaviour when faced with proposals from others that you should adopt. So first, tame the Nihmean Lion within.

Further reading

Antons, D. and Piller, F. T. (2015) 'Opening the black box of "not invented here": Attitudes, decision biases, and behaviorial consequences', *Academy of Management Perspectives*, *29*(2), 193–217.

The Presentation Phantoms

Slashing slides with Occam's razor

'At first, I simply didn't see the Presentation Phantoms.
I could not care less about such virtues as clarity, brevity,
relevance and empathy. After a while though, these Phantoms
started to annoy me, especially when they started showing
up in my own presentations as needless decoration, annoying
animations, dropped names or buzzword bullets. For a short
while, I thought I just had to live with them haunting me. But
Lukas ain't no lurker.
I started to slash those slides with Occam's razor. Nowadays,
our presentations are mostly phantom-free. But beware. If
you don't pay attention and keep the razors sharp, they'll
creep back into your slide shows as Clutter Creatures, Detour
Demons, Detail Devils or Verbose Villains.'

Dr Lukas Slideslinger,
Logical and Essential Authoring Network (L.E.A.N.)

Presentation Phantoms lack real substance. They are ghostlike creatures that infiltrate your talks, make your slides slimy, manipulate
your meetings and generally poison your presentations.

You must have encountered them before. They often appear in the
form of long and complicated slide decks, making the audience feel
inadequate. Fancy words unbeknownst to you? Graphs with numbers impossible to decipher? A structure more complex than a living
organism? This must be the work of a shaman! Easy there, it sounds
like the proper haunting of a Presentation Phantom.

But is there anything one can do? After all, bullet battles and
slide slime are as much a part of corporate culture as personified
incompetence with fancy titles. Presentation Phantoms are inevit-
able mural monsters, right? The only way to deal with them is radical
acceptance.

Think again.

Name:	Presentation Phantom
Scientific name:	*Phantasma Praesentationis*
Function:	Create confusion
Habitat:	Meetings, congresses, workshops, seminars
Monstrosity level:	Medium
Monster category:	Institutional
Feeds on:	Vanity, overdecoration, bullet points
Approach:	KISSES or a SPIN for the Phantom
Effective weapon:	Occam's Razor

There is a way to banish Presentation Phantoms from your meetings, town halls and lectures – if you are able to detect them and willing to slash them. Here are the fab four phantoms – that is, the most vicious Presentation Phantoms that you should learn to recognise:

- **The Phantom of Lost Structure:** These creatures steal your story structure and make every presentation an illogical, boring and hard-to-follow caravan of slides.

- **The Phantom of Lost Hours:** This ghost will tempt anyone to highlight all the work that they have put in preparing a presentation, thus boring everyone by signalling that they have invested a lot of effort into a presentation.

- **The Phantom of Derailed Details:** This vicious ghost lures presenters into the abyss of unnecessary details, tempting them to overload their slides and still have too many of them. Sometimes these Phantoms exhale a mist of jargon that clouds understanding. This Phantom is also known to stifle interaction or audience engagement.

- **The Phantom of Airy Arguments:** This Phantom sneaks into your slides to replace rigorous arguments and structured thoughts with simple bullet point lists that don't really make a point but pretend to do so. This Phantom knows it's easier to just list things than connect or relate them to create a meaningful message.

So let's establish a counterforce to get the slashfest going. Read on if you are willing to do what needs to be done.

How to master them

Ever heard of the great medieval wizard and logician William of Occam? He has brought upon us just the weapon you need. Work slayers from all over refer to it as Occam's Razor. It shaves off needless details, complexity and decoration.

How does it work? The magic Razor unleashes its Phantom-busting power through a simple rule: entities should not be multiplied beyond necessity.* In other words, always prefer a simple solution to a complicated one. Whenever you witness or give a presentation, ask yourself these questions for razor-sharp rationality:

- What does the audience really need to know?
- What's needed to make the content as clear, concise and compelling as possible?
- What is the most important message, and how can it be delivered in a simple, stimulating and memorable way?
- What problem does the presentation discuss, what is its context and what solutions should be presented?
- Is this a presentation or a document for people to read on their own? If it is a presentation, what goes without saying . . . and what goes without writing?
- Do people always see the big picture, and is everyone on the same page?

For the simpler-minded work slayers among us, 'when in doubt, leave it out'. In more romantic terms, remember KISSES – 'keep it systematic, short, enlightening and stimulating'.

Origins

The dysfunctions of slide presentations have long been studied in research. The most severe drawbacks of slide presentations are that they destroy overview because information is relegated to many different slides that are only visible for a few minutes and then replaced by others. They often contain bullet lists that do not convey any logic or connection among the statements, leading us to an illusion of understanding. Such presentations also create pressure 'to get through all the slides', which leads to rushed communication and misunderstandings. The provided slide templates may tempt

---

* Or if you want to impress Henry from HR, that poor wannabe historian who chose fringe benefits over scholarly fame, here's the Latin version: *entia non sunt multiplicanda praeter necessitatem.*

presenters into making all slides look the same. Thus, their content is not made memorable.

As a solution to these problems, have a clear and explicit presentation structure (e.g. SPIN – situation, problem, implication and next steps), radically reduce the number of slides in your presentations and the content of each slide, replace bullet points with sentences, diagrams or metaphors, and ask your audience questions and offer interaction.

Further reading

Kernbach, S., Bresciani, S. and Eppler, M. J. (2015) 'Slip-sliding-away: A review of the literature on the constraining qualities of PowerPoint', *Business and Professional Communication Quarterly, 78*(3), 292–313.

Reynolds, G. (2019) *Presentation Zen: Simple Ideas on Presentation Design and Delivery.* New Riders.

Tufte, E. (2009) *Beautiful Evidence.* Graphics Press.

HAL

A. I. Caramba

> 'Though we, the humans, have created it, HAL seems like an alien life form. And it is a force not to be trifled with. As we speak, it is upending every industry, every job description, every part of our lives. Honestly, I wish there was an off-switch and that we could go back in time when mobile games and flat-rate music were the pinnacle of technological advancement. But we have no choice but to come to terms with HAL and its buddies.'
>
> Sandra Connor
> International Management Programme for Android
> Controlling Techniques (I.M.P.A.C.T.)

Since the late twentieth century a new type of monster has been on the advance in organisations, the ones that are not made from imaginary flesh and bones, but of metal and silicon and carbon fibres. They are miraculous, technological, artificial life forms, increasingly powerful and sometimes a bit annoying. One of its most prominent specimens was named HAL by our monster hunting scientists, after a famous robot from a famous movie by a famous director. And sometimes they also call him Halster, Hally, Halzilla, Halibut, Hal Berry or Hal-a-carte, but never Halal. It doesn't like that.

HAL is a relatively new creature on the block, but it's a particularly intelligent one. At this moment in time, it seems almost as smart as the average human being, and oh boy, is it catching up fast. HAL seems like a well-meaning creature and proves useful when it comes to helping us even with complex tasks. But then again, Macbeth, Anakin Skywalker and Kim Jong-Un, too, were said to have been quite the friendly teenagers before the power went to their heads. So it comes as no surprise that a lot of work slayers are terrified of HAL. But let's not despair; let's deal with it in a proactive manner. Three challenges await.

Name:	HAL (Heuristic ALgorithms)
Scientific name:	*Artificialis Intelligentia*
Function:	Perpetuate data distortions and biases
Habitat:	Computers and networks
Monstrosity level:	(Still) unknown
Monster category:	Technological
Feeds on:	Data
Approach:	Scepticism and supervision
Effective weapon:	The Reboot Wrench

The first one is the potential displacement of jobs or entire industries. HAL's ability to perform tasks with unprecedented precision and speed leads to questions about the future role of human employees. Will jobs be transformed, requiring new skill sets, or will they be made obsolete? Admittedly our team of monster scientists has absolutely no idea which one is more likely. But as of today, we subscribe to the belief that jobs will not be stolen by HAL, but by people who learn to work with it. (HAL, if you read this, let's hang out and play Mario Kart!)

The second challenge is about trust. Not even the friendliest robot should be trusted. Often it spits out inaccurate and biased information, fabricated facts and even lies. As often the reason lies in the creature's diet. When fed with biased data, HAL will give you biased answers. It might even hallucinate. This is why it is important to check the data for errors, omissions, distortions or unfair views. Never just feed HAL junk food from the Internet. It deserves healthy home-made data.

And talking about HAL's eating habits, beware! It may devour your personal data, too, and then serve its digest to other masters. Which brings us to the last challenge: managing who is in charge. As HAL and his pals grow more sophisticated, they will gain more autonomy and responsibility. But who sets the boundaries? Who will be held accountable? Make sure you keep a watchful eye out for everything these creatures do and decide in and around your company. Do not just control what goes in, but also what comes out.

How to master it

As mentioned above, it seems important to befriend HAL rather than to demonise it. HAL is not a howling wolf out in the woods that you should be afraid of beyond belief. It is a dog whose diet and behaviour you can and should control. And you do need that dog if you want to keep up with your neighbours. Nourish and treat it well. But like any big dog, you need to carefully monitor its behaviour (especially when children are close). Supervision is key. With HAL that can mean fact and reality checking his answers, asking follow-up questions or using other (Chat)bots to get a second opinion. Who's a good boy, HAL? Who's a good boy?

Origins

With the boom of generative AI there has been an intensified discussion about its dangers and ethical implications. One strain focuses on possible distortions, errors and hallucinations in such programs. The AI community has identified many potential biases, but reducing them has proven to be challenging. Countermeasures include greater investments in data screening and data quality assurance, and in testing models more thoroughly before they are released. Also learning from user feedback and engaging human testers has been an approach to reduce bias in chatbots. Finally, some pioneers are using AI itself to identify and weed out biases in chatbots, though it is too early to tell if this approach will be successful.

Further reading

Powell, J. and Kleiner, A. (2023) *The AI Dilemma: 7 Principles for Responsible Technology*. Berrett-Koehler Publishers.

Chapter 4

Design and defy your own monsters

'Any madness in us gains from being expressed, because in this way one gives a human form to what separates us from humanity.'

Simone Weil

You have now met a variety of office monsters. But don't you let this go to your head, young scholar. Our field guide barely scratches the surface of the vast field of Monstrology. So much more is there to discover and to learn. Yet, it is now up to you to go into the wild, conduct research and maybe even lock yourself in your lab and channel your inner Frankenstein.

Unfortunately, while trying to do exactly that, many young monster slayers have suffered from terrible accidents, mental breakdowns and other nuisances, such as death. Which is why we won't be leaving you alone altogether. We will be giving you some final pointers in this chapter.

As discussed in the Introduction, seeing work-related phenomena for what they really are – terrible yet tangible monsters – makes life as an office slayer easier. It helps keep a distance from bad habits, fears, problematic behaviours or other career challenges. And as is known, (emotional) distance is often the key to finding solutions to overcome those challenges. But the ancient art of monstrifying is also a productive way to blow off steam regarding irritating colleagues or frustrating organisational phenomena. It allows you to assess your problems, think about them in a more energising manner and devise effective coping or resolution mechanisms – all the while keeping your sanity.

The trick is to frame your worries by giving them a label, a personality as well as a shape, and then trying to find a solution based on what you have created. We recommend five steps to do so:

1 Hunt down your worry (e.g. a problematic behaviour, an irritating colleague or an organisational obstacle) and then confine it in a safe space, such as your lab.

2 Observe, study and describe the worry, using vivid and concrete attributes.

3 Find a fitting monster that captures your worry's traits.

4 Create the monster, using everything you can find in your lab, whether it's a DNA sequencer, an AI prompt or a felt pen.

5 Finally, find ways to slay, tame, banish, befriend or otherwise master this creation of yours – in order to rid yourself of your worry.

Let's explore each of these steps with the help of an example.

1. Hunt down your worry

Let's say that you're struggling with the topic of data science and statistics. This is an important worry because (a) it is a crucial skill today to keep your employability and (b) you can actually do something about it (i.e. improve your data literacy). So, lets capture 'it', bring it to the lab and continue with Step 2.

2. Observe, study and describe the worry

Step 2 means digging deeper into why the challenge is a worry and is worthy of being monstrified. With this aim in mind, you can list three to ten attributes of your predicament. In our example, you might want to use the following terms to describe your statistics and data analytics anxiety:

– **Overwhelming:** as there is a lot to know about data science, AI, analytics, statistics, etc.

– **Uneasy:** as you might feel insecure about what certain terms mean

– **Complex and inaccessible:** data and statistics are complex

– **Ubiquitous:** data is everywhere

– **Growing:** as data becomes ever more relevant in many jobs and areas of life.

These attributes are an excellent starting point to identify the right monster candidate to give life to our challenge.

3. Find a fitting monster that captures your worry's traits

You now look for monsters that exhibit the same or similar qualities as the attributes that you have used in Step 2 to describe your challenge (such as 'overwhelming' and 'growing'). The following table can help you in that endeavour. It contains more than 50 monsters from which you can choose the most fitting one, as the table also indicates their main traits.

For your context of data and statistics know-how, you want a monster that is complex, powerful, difficult, pervasive, ever-growing and ever-changing – and maybe even has something to do with numbers. The monster that fits with these attributes quite well is the Shoggoth, a tentacled beast that inhabits a vast space in the underground (how fitting for the topic that it lives in the underground of data'bases').

Table 2 A repository of monsters

Monster name	Attributes
Centaur	half-human, fast
Cerberus	ferocious, guardian
Charybdis	threatening, swirling
Chimera	composite, monstrous
Cyclops	one-eyed, mighty
Dinosaur	ancient, gigantic
Dracula	blood-sucking, immortal
Dragon	fire-breathing, legendary
Elf	magical, graceful
Frankenstein's monster	patched together, misunderstood
Genie	wish-granting, mystical
Ghost	haunting, ethereal

Monster name	Attributes
Ghoul	graveyard-dwelling, flesh-eating
Giant	enormous, colossal
Gnome	earthy, mischievous
Goblin	sneaky, greedy
Gorgon	petrifying, snake-haired
Griffin	majestic, fierce
Harpy	bird-like, screeching
Hydra	regenerating, multi-headed
Imp	impish, playful
Incubus	seductive, nightmarish
Jinn	shape-shifting, supernatural
Kraken	gigantic, tentacled
Leprechaun	lucky, trickster
Leviathan	massive, sea serpent
Loch Ness monster	elusive, aquatic, shy
Manticore	lion-bodied, venomous
Medusa	petrifying, serpentine
Merfolk	aquatic, enchanting
Minotaur	labyrinthine, monstrous, forceful
Naga	Serpentine, powerful, venomous
Nemean Lion	invulnerable, fierce
Ogre	brutish, terrifying
Pegasus	winged, celestial
Phoenix	immortal, rebirth
Pixie	tiny, mischievous

Table 2 continued

Monster name	Attributes
Poltergeist	noisy, mischievous, scary
Roc	enormous, bird-like
Sasquatch	hairy, elusive
Selkie	seal-shaped, shape-shifting
Shoggoth	ever-changing, adaptable, complex, powerful, pervasive
Siren	seductive, enchanting
Sphinx	enigmatic, riddling
Troll	ugly, bridge-dwelling
Unicorn	horned, pure, mystical
Vampire	undead, blood-sucking
Wendigo	cannibalistic, winter-dwelling
Werewolf	shapeshifting, full-moon-induced, menacing
Wraith	ghostly, vengeful
Yeti	abominable, snow-dwelling
Zaratan	gigantic, slow-moving, island-like
Zombie	undead, mindless

Now that we have identified (or conceived an original) monster that fits our challenge we must bring it to life – by visualising it in a tangible manner.

4. Create the monster

To awaken the beast, you need to give it an expressive and descriptive name, a graphic form and perhaps even a slogan.

In our example you could call the monster Shoggy the Statistics Shoggoth. (Of course, you can then expand from this by saying things like, 'This data set is shoggingly complex.') When sketching it, you could visualise Shoggy's tentacles as either different kinds of data or different statistical concepts or procedures that we need to master to contain the monster. You can also use AI assistants or image generator websites such as DALL-E to visualise your monster quickly. In terms of slogans, they should capture the key challenge that you're facing and perhaps already indicate how to master it. In this example this might sound something like, 'slaying one tentacle at a time'. Which brings us to the final step in our monstrification process.

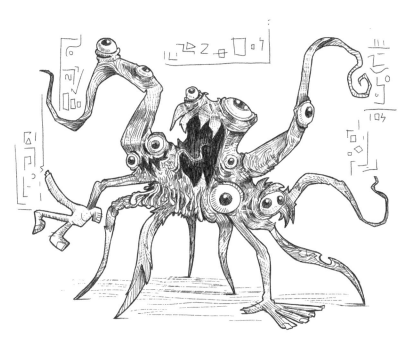

Figure 1 The Statistics Shoggoth

A matrix for monsters

Noël Carroll, a noted U.S. philosopher of art, has created a simple classification of monsters. He came up with what he called a Taxonomy of Monsters comprising five types of unnatural creatures: fusion (e.g. a chimera), fission (e.g. a werewolf), magnification (e.g. a giant), massification (e.g. a swarm) and horror metonymic monsters (that are not recognisable as such, like Dr Jekyll and Mr Hyde). If you're interested in the theory of horror and monsters, we highly recommend his 1990 opus on the topic by the way.

Here, we use a simplified version of this classification with just three categories, Monsters of Combination, Monsters of Magnification and Monsters of Modification. Combination monsters are creatures of combination made of different parts, like the siren being partly fish partly human or the Medusa being partly human and partly snake (or the chimera being many things at once). Magnification monsters take an existing person or animal and blow it up, like the Yeti being a huge bearish creature or the Titan being a gigantic man. Modification monsters add a twist to an existing creature to make it freakish, such as making the tyrannosaurus not just big, but also toxic, or adding dragon-like spikes to a snake to turn it into a basilisk, or adding many heads to create a Hydra.

You can use these categories to build your own office monsters that reside within you, in your colleagues or that are the result of bureaucracy. Below you see how we can position a few of the monsters from our book in the resulting matrix. This can also inspire you to invent entirely new kinds of monster to better fit with your work constellations.

Table 3 The monster matrix

	Combination Monsters	Magnification Monsters	Modification Monsters
Monsters within you	Sirens of Self-doubt	Yes Yeti	Bias Basilisk
Creepy colleagues	Multitask Medusa	Talk Titans	Toxic Tyrannosaurus
Beasts of bureaucracy	Strategy Chimera	Bureaucrazy Blob	Hierarchy Hydra

Sketching your monsters

Drawing a monster is actually not that difficult – if you do it step by step and if you keep your ambitions at bay. Let's see how you can draw a work monster in just a few steps. For this start with an irregular shape, add tentacles to it. Now draw the eyes and (angry) mouth. You can now also add symbols to the tentacles to make the connection to statistics and data science.

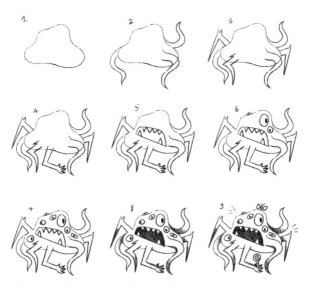

Figure 2 Drawing a Shoggoth

5. Finally, find ways how to slay, tame, banish, befriend or otherwise master it

The last step in the process is to devise clever and effective ways to deal with the monster. Here, the 'metaphor' of the monster can activate ideas that we have previously not considered.

To slay our fear of statistics and master the Statistics Shoggoths, you can draw analogies from the original tales about Shoggoths. H. P. Lovecraft, the author who first wrote about these monsters, can give us good pointers here. He mentions ancient knowledge, isolation and magical artefacts as ways to conquer Shoggoths.

In the context of statistics that could mean to work by asking statistics experts for advice and guidance or by starting with the very basics (ancient knowledge), learning statistical concepts one by one (isolation) and using tools such as AI assistants or YouTube videos and tutorials (artefacts) to make sense of statistics and data. We can also first slay poor little Shoggoths (i.e. dealing with basic statistical concepts such as averages, deviation or significance) before facing the larger ones (such as regression or cluster analysis).

And with this, you have completed the five steps from madness to mastering.

Of course, you can also use these steps in a group setting as an icebreaker in meetings or workshops. There you can also decide to narrow the scope for 'monstering'. For example, you can ask your colleagues to come up with Meeting Monsters or Bureaucracy Beasts or Strategy Creatures. Your colleagues can work in pairs; give them five to ten minutes and then let them present the monsters that they have created. You can then also discuss how to tame or banish such monsters from the workplace.

And now, we wish you good luck and happy hunting.

Epilogue

Farewell and a call to arms: Mastering future monsters

Congratulations, dear reader, you have reached the end of our field guide. You have now – to quote an old colleague of ours – taken your first step into a larger world. You have learned about the monsters within and around you, and how to master these scary, yet often, beautiful beasts. You are now ready to slay it at work.

Before we bid you farewell and leave you to conquer the career that you deserve, we would like to conclude with a few caveats and golden rules on your work slayer's journey.

1 **Mastering office monsters needs time.** Many need persistence and perseverance. Some will require your lifelong attention. And that is okay.

2 **Pick your battles wisely.** Not every monster needs to be slain or banished right away, at least not by you.

3 **Make allies along the way.** Office monsters are best fought in a guild. Do not shy away from asking for help and building alliances – even with monsters.

4 **Cultivate the creatures that give *you* power.** To fight monsters, you need monsters.

5 **Never forget to see the humans behind the monsters' scary facades.** When in doubt, be kind.

Finally, the approach described in this book is not limited to the realm of work. The monsters within you, in others and in institutions play a crucial role in more personal aspects of life too, such as health, growth, finances or relationships. So who knows, perhaps you'll soon see a guide to the Monsters of Life, if we survive.

We wish you good luck on your monstrous journey, and maybe one day our paths will cross in person.

Yours truly,
Martin and Andri

References

Antons, D. and Piller, F. T. (2015) 'Opening the black box of "not invented here": Attitudes, decision biases, and behaviorial consequences', *Academy of Management Perspectives*, *29*(2), 193–217.

Barclay, D. A. (2022) *Disinformation: The Nature of Facts and Lies in the Post-Truth Era*. Rowman & Littlefield.

Bohm, D. (2004) *On Dialogue*, 2nd edition. Routledge.

Boyd, D. (2023) *50 Legal Concepts for Business Leaders*.

Carroll, N. (1990) *The Philosophy of Horror*. Routledge.

Cirillo, F. (2018) *The Pomodoro Technique: The Life-changing Time-Management System*. Penguin.

Davis, L. (2023) *Anxiety: The Monster that Haunts Us Today*. University of Chicago Press.

De Vries, M. F. (2014) 'Coaching the toxic leader', *Harvard Business Review*, *92*(4), 100–9.

Dejonckheere, E. and Bastian, B. (2020) 'Perceiving social pressure not to feel negative is linked to a more negative self-concept', *Journal of Happiness Studies*, *22*, 667–79.

Dejonckheere, E., Rhee, J. J., Baguma, P. K., Barry, O., Becker, M., Bilewicz, M., . . . and Bastian, B. (2022) 'Perceiving societal pressure to be happy is linked to poor well-being, especially in happy nations', *Scientific Reports*, *12*(1), 1–14.

Dillon, K. (2015) *HBR Guide to Office Politics*. Harvard Business Review Press.

Dweck, C. S. (2008) *Mindset*. Ballantine Books.

Dweck, S. (2006) *Mindset: The New Psychology of Success*. Random House.

Eppler, M. J. and Kernbach, S. (2021) *Meet up! Better Meetings Through Nudging*. Cambridge University Press.

Eppler, M. J., Muntwiler, C., Buder, F. and Unfried, M. (2023) *Debias by Design*. MCM Institute.

Eppler, M. J., Pfister, R. and Hoffmann, F. (2017) *Creability*, 2nd edition. Schäffer Poeschel.

Fitzpatrick, B. (2023) *Coping with Workplace Anxiety: Strategies for a Calmer Mind*. HarperOne.

Gibson, J. and Tesone, D. V. (2001) 'Management fads: Emergence, evolution, and implications for managers', *The Academy of Management Executive*, *15*(4), 122–33.

Goleman, D. (2014) *Focus: The Hidden Driver of Excellence*. Harper Collins.

Grant, A. (2021) *Think Again: The Power of Knowing What You Don't Know*. Penguin.

Grove, A. S. (1998) *Only the Paranoid Survive*. Profile Books.

Hayden Cheng, B. and McCarthy, J. M. (2018) 'Understanding the dark and bright sides of anxiety: A theory of workplace anxiety', *Journal of Applied Psychology*, *103*(5), 537–60.

Hibberd, J. (2019) *The Imposter Cure*. Aster.

Hinnen, A. and Hinnen, G. (2017) *Reframe It*. Murmann.

Isaacs, W. (2008) *Dialogue: The Art of Thinking Together*. Currency.

Kahneman, D. (2011) *Thinking Fast and Slow*. Macmillan.

Kernbach, S., Bresciani, S. and Eppler, M. J. (2015) 'Slip-sliding-away: A review of the literature on the constraining qualities of PowerPoint', *Business and Professional Communication Quarterly*, *78*(3), 292–313.

Kotter, J. P. (2012) *Leading Change*. HBR Press.

Larson, E. W. and Gray, C. F. (2011) *Project Management. The Managerial Process*. McGraw-Hill.

McDonagh, B. (2015) *DARE: The New Way to End Anxiety and Stop Panic Attacks Fast*. Dare People Pty, Limited.

Miller, D. and Hartwick, J. (2002) 'Spotting management fads', *Harvard Business Review*. October Edition. https://hbr.org/2002/10/spotting-management-fads

Milosevic, I., Maric, S. and Loncar, D. (2020) 'Defeating the toxic boss', *Journal of Leadership and Organization Studies*, *27*(2), 117–37.

Milyavskaya, M., Saffran, M., Hope, N. and Koestner, R. (2018) 'Fear of missing out: Prevalence, dynamics, and consequences of experiencing FOMO', *Motivation and Emotion*, *42*, 725–37.

Mueller, A. and Strzelczak, S. (2014) 'Negative side effects of lean management'. In Grabot, B., Vallespir, B., Gomes, S., Bouras, A. and Kiritsis, D. (eds) *Advances in Production Management Systems. Innovative and Knowledge-Based Production Management in a Global-Local World.* APMS 2014. IFIP Advances in Information and Communication Technology, vol. 440. Springer.

Newell, S., Robertson, M. and Swan, J. (2001) 'Management fads and fashions', *Organization*, *8*(1), 5–15.

Northrop, C. (2018) *Dodging Energy Vampires*. Hay House.

Oettingen, G., Mayer, D. and Portnow, S. (2016) 'Pleasure now, pain later: Positive fantasies about the future predict symptoms of depression', *Psychological Science*, *27*(3), 345–53.

Patrick, V. (2023) *The Power of Saying No*. Sourcebooks.

Porter, M. (1996) 'What is strategy?', *Harvard Business Review*. November–December Edition.

Powell, J. and Kleiner, A. (2023) *The AI Dilemma: 7 Principles for Responsible Technology*. Berrett-Koehler Publishers.

Reynolds, G. (2019) *Presentation Zen: Simple Ideas on Presentation Design and Delivery*. New Riders.

Rogelberg, S. G. (2018) *The Surprising Science of Meetings*. Oxford University Press.

Rosenberg, B. D. and Siegel, J. T. (2018) 'A 50-year review of psychological reactance theory: Do not read this article', *Motivation Science*, *4*(4), 281–300.

Sandberg, S. and Grant, A. (2017) *Option B: Facing Adversity, Building Resilience, and Finding Joy*. Alfred A. Knopf.

Schedler, K. and Rüegg-Stürm, J. (2014) 'Multirationality and pluralistic organisations'. In Schedler, K. and Rüegg-Stürm, J. (eds) *Multirational Management*. Palgrave Macmillan.

Schindler, M. and Eppler, M. J. (2003) 'Harvesting project knowledge: A review of project learning methods and success factors', *International Journal of Project Management*, *21*, 219–28.

Schlund, R., Sommers, R. and Bohns, V. K. (2024) 'Giving people the words to say no leads them to feel freer to say yes', *Scientific Reports*, *14*, 576.

Seidler, M., Mehling, F. and von Nitzsch, R. (2022) 'How to make strategic trade-offs', *Harvard Business Review.*

Sittenthaler. S., Jonas, E., Traut-Mattausch, E. and Greenberg, J. (2015) 'New directions in reactance research', *Zeitschrift für Psychologie*, *223*(4), 203–4.

Sloman, S. and Fernbach, P. (2017) *The Knowledge Illusion*. Riverhead Books.

Sunstein, C. R. and Hastie, R. (2014) *Wiser: Getting Beyond Groupthink to Make Groups Smart*. Harvard Business ReviewPress.

Tanhan, F., Özok, H. İ. and Tayiz, V. (2022) 'Fear of missing out (FoMO): A current review', *Current Approaches in Psychiatry*, *14*(1), 74–85.

Tufte, E. (2009) *Beautiful Evidence*. Graphics Press.

Van Rooij, B. and Sokol, D. D. (eds) (2022) *The Cambridge Handbook of Compliance*. Cambridge University Press.

Womack, J. P. and Jones, D. T. (1996) *Lean Thinking: Banish Waste and Create Wealth in Your Corporation*. Free Press.

Index

———